# THE MOST BEAUTIFUL

# AND

# DANGEROUS BUSINESS

## UNCOMMON LESSONS

## FOR

## UNSTOPPABLE LEADERSHIP

### YULY GROSMAN

## Disclaimer

This book is based on my personal experiences, observations, and recollections, along with conversations I have had with growers, logistics providers, clients, and other professionals over the years. I am not an agronomist or professional grower, and this book should not be taken as technical, agricultural, legal, or financial advice.

While I have made every effort to ensure accuracy, some details, dates, and sequences may reflect my memory and perspective rather than exact records. Any resemblance to specific individuals or events beyond my personal experiences is coincidental.

The lessons and insights presented are intended for general information, storytelling, and reflection only. Readers should exercise their own judgment or seek professional guidance before applying any ideas described here. The author and publisher disclaim any liability for actions taken based on this material.

# The Most Beautiful and Dangerous Business:

# Uncommon Lessons for Unstoppable Leadership.

*"The more people touch me, the faster I will die."*
*— A truth whispered by fresh cut flowers. And a brutal reality for any business.*

Yuly Grosman

*I was trading the most extraordinary product: flowers. They accompany us throughout our lives, before we born up to generations after death, symbolizing beauty in both joy and sorrow.*

Yuly Grosman

# Acknowledgments

No leader succeeds alone.
I am deeply grateful to the mentors, colleagues, and friends who walked beside me through challenges, late nights, and impossible decisions.

**To my wife, Patricia Chin-Sweeney** — you have taught me more than you know. A true leader, a strong and brilliant woman who cares deeply about the world and works tirelessly to make it better. Your commitment to impact, to empowering women in leadership, and to being an incredible partner and mother inspire me every day. You are my partner, a friend and my heart. Your family became my family, your parents mine as well.

**To My Family** — my mother, who raised me to be who I am today, I love you even across the distance. To my father and stepfather, I am grateful to have you in my life. To my twin daughters — I know that right now, in your teenage years, you may not fully understand the lessons I'm trying to share, but one day, I hope you'll draw strength and courage from these pages and find your own power.

**To My Mother-in-Law, Carolyn Chin** — life did not give us many years together, but your daughter constantly reminds me what a remarkable woman you were. A small but powerful force who reached incredible heights — from senior executive roles at AT&T, Citibank, IBM, Reuters to leadership in U.S. government agencies and technology start-ups. You also gave your time and heart to countless nonprofits. I'm grateful we met, that you visited us in Kenya, and that we shared a safari together. Thank you for Patricia, for loving your grandson, and for our final five minutes together by your bedside — just days before your time came. You reminded me once again that nothing matters more than being human.

**To my father-in-law, Jerry** —Thank you for giving me a home when I'm away from home, and for being such a joyful, loving grandpa to our son.

**To Lior Rotem** — I'm very selective about who I call a friend, but you became one of the closest. We met in Kenya, by chance — I was running up the stairs, and you were going down. The years and distance don't matter in true friendship. Thank you for standing by me through hard moments and happy ones alike.

**To Dr. Vladimir Shchukin** — who sadly did not survive COVID-19 and never had the chance to meet our son. You were the first to know about Patricia's pregnancy and the happiest to hear the news. You were more than a doctor or surgeon — you were a man who believed in medicine before business, who could make things happen, and who lived with integrity. You became family. I miss you like I miss my grandfather. We shared laughter, stories, and holidays together in Kenya — and there was never room for politics, even when others disconnected after the war began.

**To Miki Weinberg** — my security mentor and friend. Thank you for your training, your guidance, and the quiet strength you've shared through the years.

**To Archie Alvin Athanasius** — you came to me in Kenya as a Krav Maga student, a big man with an even bigger heart. You trained hard, lost weight, and inspired others with your motivation. You became more than a student; you became a friend. I'll never forget how we shared my kitchen — I taught you how to make Russian borscht, and you taught me your Swahili shrimp recipe. I'm proud that you were among my first students to earn a 1st Dan Black Belt in Shadow Krav Maga. *Oss.*

**To Ashley Myers** — we met at my Krav Maga session. You became my student, then later I was reporting to you under a security consultancy project, and finally, we became friends. I miss our meetings, but technology makes it easier — there are no boundaries like there used to be before.

**And to all those I did not mention by name** — I know each of you, and I carry our shared memories, happiness, and sadness with me. You are part of this story too.

A special "thank you" to Tim Schulte and his team at Variance Author Services.

Most of all..

Thank you all — for believing, for standing by me, and for shaping the man and the mission behind this book.

# Contents

*Can you imagine? Living just 500 meters away from your future wife, never meeting. Five years later, she takes a picture of your phone number from a Contact Combat classes poster... and never calls. After seven years, at the right time and right place, but under the tragic circumstances of a terrorist attack where someone was killed... she calls you for security training. And that call leads to an amazing love story, with a wonderful child raised in happiness and love. This is my story.*

# Introduction:
# What You're About to Discover

I've built my life around two extremes that most people would never dare to put in the same sentence: shaping a global fresh cut flower trade, and the training of special forces in the raw, visceral art of contact combat. On the surface, these worlds seem diametrically opposed – one focused on fragile beauty, the other on brutal survival. Yet, the lessons learned in each have profoundly influenced the other, forging a unique approach to business, leadership, and resilience.

In this book, I'm not just sharing stories; I'm unveiling a philosophy. You'll discover how these seemingly disparate experiences converged to help me think strategically, lead differently, and build businesses that thrive against all odds.

We'll explore how even the most unconventional or "crazy" company name can become your greatest asset, challenging the norms and capturing attention in unexpected ways.

You'll learn what it truly means to "live flowers," to breathe their ephemeral beauty and navigate the cutthroat logistics of a multi-billion dollar industry. I'll take you deep into the heart of the hustle, sharing raw, unfiltered moments: the adrenaline-fueled anxiety of collecting cash payments and moving almost $300,000 in a backpack through the labyrinth that is the Moscow subway, every shadow a potential threat. You'll feel the gut punch of losing nearly $10,000 on a single flight, halted by customs in Ukraine due to a minor, yet catastrophic, mistake. These aren't just anecdotes; they are masterclasses in risk, adaptability, and the relentless pursuit of opportunity.

This book isn't to boast about my achievements; those you can explore on my website or LinkedIn. Instead, it's an invitation to think differently, to dissect the unconventional strategies that empowered me to transform industries and overcome seemingly insurmountable challenges.

It's for the entrepreneur who feels stuck with their startup, desperately seeking a breakthrough.

It's for the professional navigating the mid-career wilderness, searching for purpose and a new direction.

And if you've already found your stride, this book promises to unlock an entirely new perspective into the world of fresh cut flowers – a world far more complex, dangerous, and beautiful than you could ever imagine. After reading this, you won't just buy flowers; you'll appreciate the incredible human story, the daring logistics, and the profound resilience behind every delicate bloom.

But beyond the business, there's a deeply personal narrative woven into these pages. Can you imagine? Living just 500 meters away from your future wife yet never meeting. Five years later, destiny takes a bizarre turn: she sees your phone number on a Contact Combat classes poster... and never calls. Then, over seven years later, amidst the tragic circumstances of a terrorist attack where lives were lost, a different kind of call comes. In the right place, at the right time, she reaches out to you for security training. And that call, born from desperation and a need for protection, blossoms into an amazing love story, leading to a wonderful child, raised in happiness and profound love. This is my story, a testament to how even in chaos, connections are forged and new beginnings bloom.

Enjoy every moment as we peel back the layers of this beautiful and dangerous business.

---

*Is adding a 300% margin to a product theft? Or is it a brilliant business opportunity, precisely created at the right time and in the right place, delivering immense value?*

---

# Prologue:
# What Is Impact, Really?

The inspiration for this book struck me during Climate Week in New York 2024. As I moved between panels on impact investing, ESG metrics, and blended finance, a fundamental question echoed in my mind: *How do we truly measure impact?*

Most people associate impact with capital—venture funds, angel investors, or large philanthropic donations. But I'm not a traditional investor. I've never launched a fund or led a foundation. Yet, as an advisor, trainer, and entrepreneur, I've directly and indirectly helped create thousands of jobs, opened new markets, and built resilient teams in high-risk environments. This made me wonder:

***If you create profound change without writing a check, does that still make you an impact investor in your own way?***

This line of thinking led to other difficult questions.

These aren't abstract dilemmas; they are questions I've had to live and answer through my own experiences.

At just 27 years old, I found myself at a pivotal crossroads. I transitioned from the high-stakes world of security, managing riots and navigating unstable environments, to the equally competitive, yet entirely different, fresh-cut flower industry. The skills I'd developed in crisis management, strategic thinking, and reading human behavior were about to be tested in ways I never imagined.

This wasn't just a career change; it was an opportunity to reshape an entire global industry. Within just six months, I moved from field manager to general manager, leading a groundbreaking project that would position Kenya as a major player in the global flower trade. The choices I made didn't just affect market share; they profoundly impacted communities, creating thousands of jobs, funding schools, and transforming the way the world viewed Kenyan flowers. This is a story about how that transformation unfolded.

# Part I:

# Beauty and

# Danger, Where it Begins

Chapter 1:

# The Foundations of a Hustler
## From Childhood Scraps to Global Scopes

My journey began in the early 1990s, when my family embarked on a life-altering move from the vast, complex landscapes of the USSR to the ancient, promising land of Israel. It was a transition that shaped my earliest understanding of survival, adaptation, and the relentless drive to build something from nothing. The very air seemed to hum with both possibility and the echoes of past struggles, imbuing me with a deep sense of urgency.

At the tender age of 12, I began my martial arts training, not just as a hobby, but as a visceral necessity. It quickly became more than just discipline; it was a sanctuary, a school for resilience, and a silent promise of self-reliance. By age 14, the entrepreneurial spirit that would define my life had already ignited, as I launched my very first venture. The relentless drive to earn money—a profound necessity stemming from my family's status as repatriates, diligently rebuilding their lives in a new country—merged with the primal need for self-defense against bullies who, ironically, targeted me for that very status. My parents had sought to escape antisemitism and racism in the USSR, yet here I was, facing a different, more insidious form of prejudice in the very country that was supposed to offer sanctuary. The sting of that unexpected reality, the feeling of being an outsider even in a homeland, fueled a fire within me, transforming resentment into an unyielding determination.

By the time I was twelve and a half, my days were a relentless blend of working after school and dedicated martial arts practice. Every hour was an investment. These early, crucible experiences, far from being mere youthful pursuits, were the forge in which the core characteristics necessary, for later driving profound change on a global scale were hammered into being. The list of diverse jobs I held from that age until now could easily fill three A4-sized pages, each a testament to a tireless work ethic and an insatiable curiosity. Among the most pivotal were selling vibrant flowers to passing vehicles on sun-drenched Israeli roadsides, peddling intricate paintings door-to-door with a hopeful smile, and orchestrating a strategic sales project that directly contributed to my parents' ability to purchase their first apartment in Israel—a profound milestone for a family starting a new, and an early taste of the power of strategic thinking applied and resulting in real-world impact.

I'll spare you the more mundane details of my sprawling CV for now, and fast-forward to a pivotal new chapter: life after my indispensable service in the Israel Defense Forces (IDF). This period would mark another profound shift, laying the groundwork for the extraordinary paths ahead.

## *Learned Lesson: The Power of Adversity as Fuel*

*Your earliest struggles are not roadblocks; they are the foundational fuel for your future resilience and ambition. The very challenges you face—be it financial hardship, discrimination, or the need for self-defense—instill a unique drive and resourcefulness that formal education rarely provides. Embrace these "unconventional" early experiences, for they equip you with an innate hunger for success and a distinct perspective that will differentiate you in any market. Necessity truly is the mother of invention, and hardship is the forge of extraordinary capability.*

# Chapter 2:

# Forged in Fire

## Security, Conflict, and the Art of De-escalation

My transition into the world of professional security coincided with one of Israel's most tumultuous periods: the Second Intifada, or Al-Aqsa Intifada, which raged from 2000 to 2005. The nation was gripped by a relentless wave of terrorist attacks. Extremist organizations systematically deployed suicide bombers to target the most vulnerable public spaces – bustling buses, crowded shopping malls, vibrant nightclubs, and ordinary city streets. These horrific events cast a long, dark shadow, keeping the entire population in a constant, palpable state of stress and fear for many agonizing years. The air itself seemed thick with tension, and vigilance became a shared national burden.

During this intense period, I began my work as a security officer in one of Israel's major government hospitals. This wasn't merely a job; it was a front-row seat to the rawest of human emotions and conflicts. Starting as a vigilant guard at the entrance gate, observing every face, every gesture, I steadily climbed the ranks, moving into increasingly sensitive and critical positions within the hospital's complex security apparatus. It was also during this tumultuous time that Prime Minister Ariel Sharon made the pivotal, often controversial, decision to construct the West Bank separation barrier, a monumental project designed with one overriding objective: *to stem the tide of relentless attacks*. However, building a barrier of that magnitude was not an overnight task. In the interim, the hospital, like much of the country, became a microcosm of the daily threats and simmering tensions that permeated Israeli society. Riots, volatile arguments, and even violent confrontations between patients, their distraught families, and overworked healthcare staff became a distressingly common occurrence, turning a place of healing into a battleground.

Conflicts would often ignite for a myriad of reasons, some seemingly mundane, others deeply ingrained. There was the understandable frustration over agonizingly long wait times to see a doctor, pushing already stressed individuals to their breaking point. More gravely, deep-seated disputes between "Hamulas" (large Arabic families), rooted in matters of pride, complex business dealings, or entrenched family honor, could explode. What might begin as a seemingly small, contained altercation could spiral terrifyingly quickly into full-blown knife fight, sometimes resulting in a terrifying surge of 30 to 90 family members descending upon the hospital, intent on "settling" the matter after their relatives were injured and brought in for treatment. Managing these escalating situations required more than just physical presence; it demanded psychological acuity. Navigating this chaotic, often life-threatening environment was immensely challenging, but it was also an unparalleled, profoundly educational experience. I didn't just learn the protocols of physical security or how to handle a situation or avoid using a weapon; I developed acute analytical skills, learning to read situations, anticipate threats, and predict human behavior under duress.

Crucially, I honed the critical ability to negotiate, control, and de-escalate extreme aggression in real-time, often using words rather than force. These hard-won skills, sharpened under immense pressure, proved to be invaluable years later when I moved to Africa, where I would begin training corporations on precisely how to navigate uncertainty, manage complex risks, and maintain control through sophisticated communication and de-escalation strategies. The hospital, in essence, became my first business school.

### Learned Lesson: Chaos as the Ultimate Classroom

*The most intense and chaotic environments are often the richest training grounds for essential business skills. Don't shy away from high-stress situations; embrace them. Whether it's managing a crisis, de-escalating a heated conflict, or simply observing human behavior under pressure, these experiences forge invaluable analytical capabilities, negotiation prowess, and the ability to maintain composure when everything around you is unraveling. These are not just security skills; they are the bedrock of strategic leadership and effective management in any industry, preparing you to thrive where others falter.*

# Chapter 3:

# The Pivot

## From Crisis Zones to Entrepreneurial Heights

Many of the most profound career shifts don't start with a bold plan. They begin with a quiet whisper: a growing sense that your skills belong somewhere else. This chapter is about that whisper becoming a roar.

Even during my demanding years immersed in the world of security, my innate entrepreneurial drive refused to be suppressed. It was a constant hum beneath the surface, an internal engine always seeking new avenues. In fact, I covertly founded a few businesses along the way, nurturing them in the margins of my intense security work, though those specific ventures aren't the primary focus of this unfolding narrative. They served as vital incubators for my business acumen, experiments in resourcefulness.

After almost six grueling years of living and working under the unrelenting pressure of constant stress, the weight of constant vigilance, at the age of 26, I made a decisive, life-altering decision: I quit security. The time had come; my spirit yearned for a new career, a different path, one that promised creation rather than constant defense. The decision wasn't made lightly, but with a deep conviction that my unique skillset was destined for another arena.

Interestingly, the very entrepreneurial side of my life that I initially wanted to gloss over, perhaps considering it a mere side-hustle, was precisely what paved the way, almost serendipitously, for my next significant role. While deeply immersed in security—a profession that, I must add, didn't pay nearly well enough to match the inherent risks and demands, leaving me in a constant financial stretch—I was simultaneously juggling two additional jobs just to make ends meet. I was meticulously working as a barman's assistant at bustling wedding venues, a stark contrast to my daily routine, and diligently cleaning offices in the quiet, late hours, often well into the night.

But the true adventure, the real igniting spark that would set my future course, began when I embarked on importing computer accessories from China to Israel, successfully distributing them to large corporations, including burgeoning international tech startups. This was a deep dive into global supply chains and sales on a scale I hadn't touched before.

The pivotal turning point arrived with a jolt, triggered by a story that captivated national news and stirred a profound sense of unease within me: a Russian-speaking babysitter caught on a home camera cruelly abusing a baby. This horrifying event didn't just shock me; it ignited a powerful, personal challenge within me to find a new, genuinely easy-to-install hidden camera solution that parents could seamlessly integrate into their homes for peace of mind and protection. That urgent, purpose-driven quest ultimately led me to a dedicated night-shift purchasing role at my own burgeoning business, where I tirelessly scoured the digital marketplaces of Alibaba, not just for hidden gadgets, but for new opportunities waiting to be discovered, for unmet needs crying out for innovative solutions. As promised, I won't dive into the intricate details of that specific entrepreneurial odyssey right now, but its impact on my skills and mindset was profound.

However, I will emphasize this: that diverse and dynamic entrepreneurial background, built on grit, resourcefulness, and a willingness to explore uncharted territories, gave me an undeniable edge when I stumbled upon a job listing for a field manager position at an export fresh-cut flowers company. One of the key skills they desperately needed, clearly articulated in the job description, was in purchasing and sales—a role that surprisingly, was a perfect, almost uncanny, match for my accumulated, unconventional experience. It felt like fate.

In October 2005, I walked into the interview, armed with an unusual resume but a wealth of real-world experience. I landed the role on a trial basis, accepting a very modest salary, seeing it as an investment in a new future. My initial job was deceptively simple: drive around Israel, visit flower growers, meticulously gather information on available flowers, and report back to the office, where someone else would then process the data and make the decisions.

Flowers! I confidently believed I knew everything about flowers! During my middle and high school years, I'd earned my stripes selling flowers on the roadside. I could rattle off their characteristics: they were big, they were red, pink, or white, with or without leaves. Some emanated gorgeous scents, while others, frankly, stunk. And a crucial, painful lesson: some would wilt faster than I could even manage to sell them to impatient drivers waiting at red lights. I was, in my youthful mind, a PRO! Oh, how much more I had to learn.

### *Learned Lesson: Your "Side Hustles" Are Your Superpowers*

*Never dismiss any experience, especially those borne out of necessity or passion, as merely a "side hustle" or irrelevant. The skills honed while juggling multiple jobs—whether it's bartending, cleaning offices, or importing obscure goods—build a unique, multidisciplinary skillset that traditional career paths often fail to provide. These diverse experiences cultivate resourcefulness, negotiation tactics, market understanding, and an unparalleled work ethic. They often become the hidden advantage that paves the way for unexpected opportunities and equips you to thrive in entirely new industries. Your most unconventional experiences are often your most valuable assets.*

Reflection and Wrap-up:

Sometimes, the path forward is hidden in plain sight—inside the jobs we undervalue or hide from our resumes. The overlooked chapters of your life may be the blueprint to your next reinvention. This chapter is proof: the pivot point in your story may not be dramatic—it may be subtle. The seed of a global transformation might already live in the side hustle you're doing tonight, the conversation that disturbed you this morning, or the job you take just to survive. Stay curious. Stay alert. That next step will call you when you're ready to hear it.

# Chapter 4:
# The Unseen Complexities

Mastering the Delicate Dance of the Flower
Business

What looks effortless on the surface often hides an invisible
world of complexity, risk, and expertise. Flowers taught me
this. Fast.

After just one intense week of driving around,
meeting local flower producers—the dedicated farmers
behind the blooms, whose hands were as calloused as their
spirits were resilient—I swiftly realized that flowers were
infinitely more complex and intricate than my roadside sales
had ever revealed. My youthful confidence in my *"PRO"*
status evaporated like the morning dew. They weren't just
botanical names from a textbook; they came with specific
prices that fluctuated wildly with demand, varying vase life
(both before and after meticulous packaging that could add
days or steal hours), and most critically, they were living
organisms that could fall ill! This revelation was a profound
shift in my understanding of a product I thought I knew so
well.

I quickly grasped that when flowers became
susceptible to disease, it wasn't merely a matter of affecting
profits; it could completely derail entire business plans,

leading to catastrophic losses that rippled through the entire supply chain. In this high-stakes environment, only competitors who possessed the foresight to predict, and the agility to navigate these unpredictable uncertainties could truly pull ahead, turning potential disaster into strategic advantage. This was no longer just about selling; it was about scientific understanding, meticulous planning, and lightning-fast adaptation.

Over the next few intense weeks, I meticulously split my working days. Part of my time was spent on the road, engaging directly with growers, building rapport, and assessing their crops—learning the nuances of soil, climate, and cultivation. The other, often longer part was spent in the office, immersed in thousands of pictures of flowers and green fillers, relentlessly studying to memorize their types, names, and countless varieties. Each image, each new name, was a step deeper into a fascinating, fragile world. The long hours and undeniably low salary didn't deter me. A powerful gut feeling—sharpened and refined by my years in security and my earlier entrepreneurial forays into everything from paintings to electronics—persisted, whispering that I was unequivocally on the right path, and that a transformative future was tantalizingly close. This wasn't just a job; it was an apprenticeship in an extraordinary, living ecosystem.

I was now deeply immersed in the world of trading the most extraordinary product imaginable: flowers. They are woven into the very fabric of human experience, accompanying us throughout our lives, from the moments before we are born, celebrating new life and hopeful beginnings, to generations after our passing, marking loss, remembrance, and enduring love. They are timeless symbols of beauty in both profound joy and aching sorrow, a universal language spoken across cultures.

I'll be honest: it was no easy task to commit to memory the fifteen different names and varieties of white roses alone (and today, there are many, many more). At that initial point, they all looked absolutely identical to me. They were white, they were roses, and they simply came in different lengths—mostly 40 cm to 60 cm, as per our company's specific client needs. The subtle distinctions that differentiated a Acito from a 'Vendela' seemed utterly imperceptible to my untrained eye, yet I knew mastering them was critical.

Our company operated with several specialized refrigerated trucks and a vast warehouse meticulously equipped with temperature-controlled storage, designed for both delicate horticulture and broader agriculture products. Flowers would be precisely collected by our trucks, adhering strictly to the intricate logistical plans crafted by another manager. Once at the warehouse, they would be carefully cooled, subjected to rigorous inspection, and packed according to both exacting company and diverse client requirements, before embarking on their journey to Ben Gurion International Airport. That is, if we were lucky enough to secure precious space with an airfreight agent—another critical skill I would soon learn to master. Cultivating and maintaining strong, almost familial relationships with airfreight agents would become one of the most crucial abilities, capable of either propelling your business forward with lightning speed or leaving you agonizingly behind in a race against time and decay.

I was never scared of fieldwork, of getting my hands dirty, regardless of my specific role or the position I held. This hands-on approach, ingrained from my earliest days, proved invaluable. And it turned out that helping to pack flowers myself was one of the smartest decisions I made. Physically handling different types of flowers, working shoulder-to-shoulder with seasoned experts who could identify a sick stem or a perfect bud by touch alone, allowed me to learn names, shapes, and varieties with astonishing speed. The hands-on process of meticulously examining flowers for subtle bugs, imperfections, or early signs of disease became a crash course, fast-tracking my knowledge acquisition beyond any theoretical training. It was in these moments, amidst the scent of damp earth and fresh petals, that I truly began to understand the fragile power of the product.

This is an opportune moment to clarify some essential industry terminology:

- **Fillers:** These are the unsung heroes of floristry — various plants, grasses, and smaller flowers that florists skillfully use to complement and enhance larger, focal blooms in bouquets. They are designed to add volume, texture, and often a lush, extravagant feel. These fillers can range from common plants found right in your backyard to specially propagated varieties for which growers pay significant royalties, reflecting intellectual property and meticulous cultivation.

- **The Unconventional Value:** Could you imagine that even a simple weed growing by the sidewalk can find its way into a high-end bouquet, sometimes priced at a staggering $500, if a truly creative florist deems it perfect for a discerning politician, a celebrated celebrity's birthday, or a grand event? This highlights the immense, often unseen, value in perceived 'insignificance' when paired with vision, proving that innovation and a fresh perspective can redefine market value.

My experience in founding a food production line, *The Taste of Home Kenya*, was not an act of magic but a direct application of this evolving mindset. It was a potent combination of creative vision, practical business experience gleaned from flowers, and a profound desire to make a tangible change in people's lives by addressing a deeply personal need. *The Taste of Home Kenya* was a testament to this philosophy: the beauty of a flower, infused with the comforting scent of raspberry, evoking the missing taste of home. It was one more perfect combination, timed precisely for the right market and the right place, demonstrating that unexpected synergies can yield extraordinary results.

### Learned Lesson: The Depth of Hidden Complexity

*Every industry, no matter how simple it appears on the surface, harbors a profound depth of complexity. True mastery comes not from superficial knowledge, but from diving deep into the nuances, the science, the logistics, and even the vulnerabilities of your product or service. Embrace the steep learning curve. The more intimately you understand the intricacies—from the biology of a flower to the subtle art of airfreight negotiation—the more effectively you can anticipate challenges, outmaneuver competitors, and uncover hidden opportunities for innovation and profit. Complexity isn't a barrier; it's a competitive advantage for those willing to truly learn.*

Reflection and Wrap-up:

What seems insignificant—like a weed, a packing job, or a scent—can carry emotional power, market value, and global potential. If you slow down and study the system deeply, you'll begin to see the patterns others miss.

You're not selling flowers. You're managing biology, culture, supply chains, and emotion. The lesson? What looks simple is rarely simple. Leaders who slow down to master complexity—especially in emotional, time-sensitive markets—are the ones who win.

---

*Any truly successful entrepreneur or seasoned salesperson reading this understands that empathy and genuine sympathy — not forced friendliness or calculated charm — are the bedrock upon which real doors open and enduring business relationships flourish.*

---

# Chapter 5:
# The Architect of Growth

## How a 27-Year-Old Sparked a Cross-Continental Transformation

It's easy to underestimate someone because of age or title. But transformation doesn't require a senior role — just the guts to ask better questions, build real trust, and act where others hesitate.

Now, you may be wondering how a 27-year-old field manager, ostensibly at the bottom of the ladder, could go on to found and lead a groundbreaking project that connected continents, reshaping an entire industry and leaving an indelible mark on global trade. The leap from daily grind to international impact might seem impossible, but it was a journey paved with relentless curiosity and an eagerness to connect.

Just a few months into my initial role, I had already become deeply involved in various, seemingly disparate aspects of the company. My responsibilities quickly expanded beyond basic field management to include hands-on packing assistance, intricate logistics coordination, and even occasionally negotiating crucial prices with growers—a task typically reserved for more senior personnel. By this point, I could identify several types of roses and countless other flowers with an almost uncanny 99% certainty, a testament to my immersive learning approach and hours of dedicated study. My confidence grew not from titles, but from genuine competence.

Crucially, this period was also when I truly began to forge closer, more authentic relationships with the flower growers themselves. I understood that the heart of the business lay not just in the product, but in the people cultivating it. My accumulated experience in sales—from the early days of modeling to the relentless grind of door-to-door sales at 14, coupled with the refined social skills honed while co-owning a bustling nightclub—all proved incredibly handy. I wasn't just talking business; I was genuinely connecting. While my wonderful wife may playfully tease me and call me an "old man" now, back then I didn't just know the growers by name, but also their children and, in some cherished cases, even their grandchildren's birthdays. I learned about their struggles, their hopes, their families. Any truly successful entrepreneur or seasoned salesperson reading this understands that empathy and genuine sympathy—not forced friendliness or calculated charm—are the bedrock upon which real doors open and enduring business relationships flourish. This human connection, built on mutual respect and understanding, proved to be an invaluable currency, laying the groundwork for the audacious projects that lay ahead.

### *Learned Lesson: Human Connection as Your Greatest Asset*

*In any business, especially one aiming for global impact, your most powerful currency is genuine human connection. Beyond transactions and data, cultivating empathy, understanding, and personal relationships with partners, suppliers, and even competitors will open doors that remain closed to others. It's not about forced friendliness, but about truly seeing and valuing the people you interact with. Authentic relationships build trust, foster collaboration, and create an invaluable network that can propel your vision forward in ways no spreadsheet ever could.*

### Reflection and Wrap-up:

Impact isn't earned through hierarchy. It's earned through care. If you understand people—their motivations, struggles, and joys—you'll always have influence that outpaces your title.

Never underestimate the leverage that comes from relationships. Competence opens the door—but connection makes it swing wide open. If you want to grow something across continents, start by growing something real with the people right in front of you.

---

*As long as you possess unique knowledge, an acute observation, or a critical insight, you can unlock disproportionate value and make more money than your competitors.*

---

# Chapter 6:
# Global Ambitions and Market Realities

## Decoding the World of International Flower Trade

To truly play on the global stage, you need more than ambition—you need to decode the systems, cultures, and quiet signals that shape markets. This chapter opens the curtain on a world few ever see.

The company I joined was a complex ecosystem, structured around three intimately intertwined business models, each with its own unique challenges and opportunities:

• **Exporting Fresh Cut Flowers from Israel:** This was the primary focus, leveraging Israel's advanced agricultural technology and diverse flora to supply international markets. It meant navigating highly perishable goods and tight deadlines.

• **Exporting Vegetables from Israel to Russia and Ukraine:** This diversified our portfolio, utilizing sea freight for less time-sensitive, bulk commodities. It broadened our logistical expertise and market reach.

• **Importing Food Products from Russia and Ukraine:** This was a strategic move to target a significant niche—the almost 10% of Israel's citizens who are Russian speakers—and distribute culturally relevant food products within Israel. This venture required a deep understanding of consumer preferences and local distribution networks.

My initial immersion was primarily in the flower business. Beyond the exports from Israel, the company also actively purchased flowers from powerhouse growers in Ecuador and Colombia, known for their high-quality, large-headed roses. We also bought flowers directly at the bustling Flower Auction in Aalsmeer, Holland, the undisputed nerve center of the global flower trade—a place where fortunes could be made or lost in minutes. The majority of our meticulously cultivated exports found their way to the vast and eager markets of the former USSR region, including Russia, Kazakhstan, Ukraine, and Uzbekistan. There was also a smaller, but strategically important, market presence in the USA.

In Russia, flowers aren't just a commodity; they are a profound cultural pillar, an essential part of daily life and every significant milestone. It's a land where a man buys flowers for his mother, his wife, his girlfriend, and even several lovers on a regular basis—whether for birthdays, holidays, or, most profoundly, on Women's Day (March 8), when the demand for blooms reaches astronomical levels. The tradition of gifting flowers was deeply rooted in Soviet culture, a vibrant thread connecting generations. Every child entering the first grade on September 1st brings a bouquet of fresh flowers to their teacher, a symbol of new beginnings, and they do the same on the last day of school before summer vacation—a gesture of gratitude. This ingrained cultural practice created an endlessly robust and high-volume market.

As long as you possess unique knowledge, an acute observation, or a critical insight, you can unlock disproportionate value and make more money than your competitors. This was a truth I learned to exploit.

Russian women especially favored large roses with long stems (at least 60 cm) and impressive, full heads. Today, with precise metrics, I can tell you the head size should be at least 8–10 cm in height, a clear standard of quality. But back then, to my still-learning eye, I simply referred to them as "very big," a qualitative descriptor that still conveyed the desired grandeur.

The largest producer of these specific types of highly sought-after roses was Ecuador, although some premium varieties were also grown in Holland, often under more controlled, greenhouse conditions. There was often a subtle, yet significant, confusion among buyers regarding the true origin and specific qualities of these flowers—a confusion that as I would later discover and strategically leverage, allowed for increased revenue for those who understood the nuances and could guide the market.

Now that you understand some of the technical aspects of the product and its market, let's talk about what truly keeps you in the business, year after year, cycle after cycle. To remain fiercely competitive and capture significant market share, you need to reliably supply those coveted long-stem roses with large heads, at least 60 cm in length, precisely cut at stage 3, and crucially, boasting an exceptional long vase life. Before diving into the specific circumstances that led me to the unexpected and transformative landscapes of Africa, I need to explain one more critical aspect that underpins the entire flower trade: the cut stage. This seemingly small detail holds the key to profit, quality, and market dominance.

### Learned Lesson: Opportunity Hides in Plain Sight

*Beyond the obvious, true business opportunities often reside in overlooked complexities, cultural nuances, or even market confusion. Learn to identify subtle distinctions in products, understand the deep-seated cultural drivers of demand, and recognize where information asymmetry exists. Those who master these "hidden secrets" —whether it's the exact cut stage of a flower or the specific cultural preference of a market—can position themselves to create immense value, secure higher margins, and stay ahead of the competition. Your ability to observe and act on what others miss is your most potent advantage.*

**Reflection and Wrap-up:**

**The power in any product lies not just in how it's made, but in how deeply you understand who it's for—and why. Cultural context is often your sharpest competitive edge. What you know matters. But how well you know your customer—and the unspoken patterns of their world— matters more. Study culture as closely as you study product. That's where the margins are hiding.**

# Chapter 7:
# The Cut Stage
## Precision, Perishability, and Market Demands

Sometimes, the smallest detail is the sharpest wedge for impact. This is the story of how understanding one technical nuance—cut stage—helped unlock an empire.

As simple as it sounds, the cut stage is an absolutely crucial, foundational element to the multi-billion-dollar flower trade—a variable that dictates profitability, market acceptance, and the very viability of a shipment. When roses are growing, their heads open at different, precise stages, a delicate process influenced by a complex ballet of factors: the specific variety of the rose, its stem length, prevailing weather conditions, the precise target market for export, and even the unique altitude or sea level of the farm where it's cultivated.

The cut stage, in essence, refers to how open the flower is at the exact moment it is harvested from the plant. This isn't arbitrary; it's a science.

• Cut Stage 1: Roses at this stage are very tightly closed, often appearing almost like small, hard buds. They promise longevity, but lack immediate visual impact to the viewer.
• Cut Stage 5: These are fully open roses, magnificent in their immediate bloom. However, they are far from ideal for

export. Their vase life is significantly shorter, and they are inherently more vulnerable to diseases and physical damage during the rigors of long-distance transportation. They are a fleeting beauty, not a durable commodity.

Understanding this nuanced distinction was a game-changer in navigating different international markets and fulfilling client expectations. For example, discerning European supermarkets often prefer roses that are still closed or almost closed, typically corresponding to a smaller head size and harvested at cut stage 1. They prioritize maximum vase life for their consumers. In stark contrast, our demanding Russian clients, driven by a cultural preference for immediate grandeur, preferred cut stage 3, where the roses are visibly more open, showcasing more of their inherent beauty upon arrival. This deep understanding of market-specific preferences was not just helpful; it was the difference between a successful sale and a devastating claim.

### Learned Lesson: The Precision of Understanding Your Product

*True mastery in business isn't just about knowing what you sell; it's about understanding its every nuance, its vulnerabilities, and its optimal presentation for each unique market. Ignorance of critical product details, like the "cut stage" of a flower, can lead to catastrophic losses, while deep knowledge unlocks bespoke solutions and competitive advantages. Invest time in understanding the smallest technical details of your product or service, as these often hold the key to unlocking new markets, satisfying specific client needs, and ultimately, ensuring your long-term success.*

**Reflection and Wrap-up:**

**In high-stakes markets, deep product knowledge is not a bonus—it's a requirement. Understanding small differences means winning big. Markets reward precision. The deeper your insight into the unseen mechanics of what you sell, the further your reach—and the stronger your reputation.**

# Chapter 8:
# Back to the Israeli Frontline

## The Unseen Pressures of Domestic Sourcing

Back home, the battlefield looked different—but the stakes were just as high. This is where I learned that even your own backyard can become the hardest front to fight on.

By late 2005 and early 2006, I had been working for the company for several intense months. While my official title might have still been "field guy" with a "trial salary," the reality was far more demanding and encompassing. I was by then, essentially doing most of the crucial tasks: grueling fieldwork under the scorching sun, navigating complex purchasing decisions, and even engaging in the delicate dance of price negotiations with growers. My days often stretched into the long, silent hours of the night, involved in meticulously packing flowers. On several occasions, I even joined the truck drivers, hurtling through the pre-dawn darkness to deliver boxes to the sprawling cargo area of Ben Gurion Airport, where I began strategically building crucial relationships with the often-elusive airfreight agents. These were the gatekeepers of global logistics, and their goodwill could make or break a shipment.

Most of the flowers we exported during this period were still primarily sourced directly from Israel. We maintained relationships with around 10 to 15 dedicated rose growers, and many more who cultivated the myriad of other flowers and green fillers that completed our orders. However, these local growers, despite their dedication, struggled constantly to produce enough roses to consistently meet our escalating demand, especially in the face of competition from private exporters and the significant, government-supported company Agresko, which eventually, and quite dramatically, collapsed under its own weight.

---

Gypsophila can release irritant compounds, especially when dried or heated, and is known to cause skin, eye, or respiratory irritation in some cases.

---

The challenges were multifaceted and relentless, forming a perfect storm that threatened the very core of our domestic supply:

• Scorching Heat: The relentless Israeli sun and high temperatures caused the delicate flowers to open far too quickly. Instead of achieving the ideal length of 60 cm with a perfect cut stage 3, most flowers prematurely reached only 40 cm with smaller, less desirable heads. This was a constant battle against nature's clock.

• Botrytis (Fungus): The humid conditions, coupled with understandable but ultimately detrimental cost-saving measures implemented by some growers, resulted in a widespread proliferation of botrytis, an insidious fungal infection that seriously impacted flower quality, often turning perfectly good stems/flowers/petals into unsellable waste overnight. This was an invisible enemy, tirelessly undermining our efforts

### *Learned Lesson: Understanding the Ecosystem of Your Supply*

*Success in a supply-chain business is not just about moving product; it's about deeply understanding and proactively managing the entire ecosystem that produces it. External factors — like weather, political decisions, or even the practices of your suppliers — can dramatically impact your product's quality and your business's viability.*

*Don't just buy; engage with your suppliers, understand their challenges, and anticipate environmental or economic shifts. Proactive engagement with your supply chain allows you to mitigate risks and innovate solutions before they become catastrophic.*

### Reflection and Wrap-up:

**Working harder isn't always the answer — working smarter with full ecosystem awareness is. What you don't see in your supply chain can — and will — hurt you. Anticipate the cracks before they turn into a collapse.**

# Chapter 9:

# The Invisible Enemy and the Quest for Profit

## Confronting Botrytis and Operational Pressures

Sometimes the threat isn't what's visible—it's what's hiding in plain sight. And that threat has a name: Botrytis.

For those unfamiliar with botrytis, let me make it simple, yet paint a vivid picture: if you've ever bought roses, you've probably unknowingly encountered it. Have you ever noticed some petals on your beautiful bouquet turning yellow or brown, or feeling suspiciously soft and mushy to the touch, almost like they're melting? That's the work of botrytis, often referred to as gray mold. It's an insidious fungus that often begins as a tiny, almost invisible dot, a microscopic imperfection hidden deep inside the flower head while it's still thriving in the seemingly pristine environment of the greenhouse.

If the flower isn't meticulously treated in time, or if the crucial cold chain during transportation is broken—even for a short period—this tiny, dormant dot can explode into a visible, destructive force. It can grow rapidly, infecting not just one stem, but thousands, or even hundreds of thousands, of flowers within a single shipment. Worse, botrytis doesn't respect boundaries; it can spread rampantly during transport, cross-contaminating entire shipments, potentially destroying everything in its path and turning a multi-thousand-dollar cargo into a total loss.

And it wasn't just mold. In some extreme cases, overheated flowers might also pose a direct danger. I recall a concerning incident where an employee sustained a facial burn or severe irritation after exposure to overheated Gypsophila (baby's breath), likely due to the plant releasing irritants when subjected to high temperatures. Gypsophila, though seemingly innocuous, can release irritant compounds, especially when dried or heated, and is known to cause skin, eye, or respiratory irritation in some cases—a detail rarely considered by the end consumer.

## Making Money: The Core Principle

I'm not quite ready to disclose the exact revenue figures or the painful losses from my early days in the flower business yet, but we're heading there, piece by detailed piece. One profound truth I've learned and always adhere to is this: if you find yourself unable to make money—if the profit margins are simply not there, or if they are eroding—you must instinctively do one of two things.

First, find a way to radically reduce costs without ever sacrificing the quality that defines your brand. Or second, innovate a product or service that the market desperately needs and is willing to pay a premium for. There is no middle ground in long-term viability.

The biggest, most pivotal change for our operation truly began to unfold at the start of 2006. At the end of 2005 and into early 2006, several domestic events converged, creating an undeniable pressure point. Once again, that familiar gut feeling resurfaced—that internal compass, sharpened by years in high-stakes security, or perhaps it was my rapidly growing, intuitive understanding of local governance, agricultural policy, and the deeply ingrained mentality around the flower industry in Israel. The writing on the wall was becoming increasingly clear.

### Learned Lesson: The Relentless Pursuit of Profitability

*Profitability is not a luxury; it's the lifeblood of your business, especially in volatile markets. When facing shrinking margins, don't just hope for better times. Instead, relentlessly pursue two core strategies: cost optimization without compromising quality, or product/service innovation that creates new market demand. Standing still or ignoring the signs of financial strain is a death sentence. Always be prepared to adapt, pivot, and proactively seek new avenues for value creation.*

**Reflection and Wrap-up:**

Mold, heat, or hidden microscopic enemies—business is always fighting the rot before the bloom. Flowers rot fast—but so do margins. Your success depends on how quickly you respond to decay, wherever it hides.

# Chapter 10:
# Converging Crises
## Manpower, Climate, and the Rise of Claims

### The Pressures Begin to Mount

The pressures on our domestic flower supply were mounting from multiple directions—a perfect storm gathering over the Israeli agricultural landscape. At the time, most of our flowers were sourced locally, but the very infrastructure that supported this sourcing model was beginning to erode. Labor shortages, extreme weather, and declining product quality were pushing us toward an inflection point.

### Foreign Manpower: The Human Cost of Production

A significant and often underexamined factor in our supply chain was the labor force. The vast majority of the fieldwork on Israeli flower farms was carried out by foreign workers—primarily from Thailand, and to a lesser extent, the Philippines and Gaza. These workers labored under intense conditions, from sunrise to nightfall, tending to delicate crops in greenhouses that turned into ovens under the Mediterranean sun.

They were involved in every stage of the process: preparing soil, maintaining greenhouse infrastructure, planting, watering, and harvesting. Their labor was essential, yet often taken for granted. While not always stemming from malice, cost-cutting by some growers led to inhumane working conditions—overcrowded housing, lack of proper sanitation, and dangerously long hours. Eventually, the press and law enforcement caught on. Several high-profile investigations and media stories accused certain growers of gross negligence, shining an unflattering light on the industry's hidden backbone.

## Middle East Weather Conditions: The Ecological Toll

Simultaneously, Israel was in the grip of an extreme, multi-year drought. The Sea of Galilee—Israel's largest freshwater reservoir—had dropped to perilously low levels. The government responded by raising water prices dramatically. These costs fell heavily on agricultural producers, many of whom were already struggling.

Flower farming is delicate and unforgiving. Roses, in particular, require stable hydration, temperature, and shade to grow to the ideal length and bloom at the right cut stage. The drought, combined with skyrocketing water costs, created a situation where flowers were maturing too fast under harsh conditions, developing shorter stems and smaller heads.

These changes weren't subtle—they directly impacted marketability. Most of our exports were no longer meeting the stringent quality expectations of international buyers, particularly those in Russia, Eastern Europe, and North America.

## Trust Erodes: The Rise of Claims

As these issues compounded, claims from international clients surged. What were once occasional quality concerns became weekly occurrences. Buyers reported botrytis outbreaks, undersized stems, or heads that opened too quickly and didn't last in vases.

To the uninitiated, a "claim" might sound like a bureaucratic inconvenience. But in the flower business, it's a high-stakes alarm bell. A claim typically arrives as an urgent complaint or formal request for a refund or credit based on poor quality or noncompliance with agreed specifications.

This is especially critical in floriculture, where the product is highly perishable. There's no time to return flowers or conduct long investigations. By the time a client files a claim, the flowers are already dead—or worse, discarded before ever making it to store shelves. Claims aren't just about product—they're about broken trust, lost customers, and eroded brand reputation.

## Understanding Risk and Responsibility

Most of our clients operated on C&F (Cost and Freight) terms. This meant that we covered the cost of the flowers and the international shipping—but not insurance. Due to their perishability, flowers are rarely insured. If a shipment failed, we bore the financial loss.

Some clients worked on FOB (Free on Board) terms, meaning our responsibility ended the moment the flowers were loaded onto the plane. But even under FOB, the pressure to deliver quality never went away. In either case, the exporter had to decide how much margin they were willing to sacrifice in the event of damage or complaints.

Let me simplify it: if I bought a stem from a grower for $0.20 and added $0.15 for expenses and margin, the FOB price might be $0.35. That's what I would charge my client up to the airport gate. Under C&F, I would add the airfreight and other international logistics costs on top. So if a client made a claim, I might be on the hook for the entire amount—unless I could prove the damage happened after the transfer of risk. But proving that? Rarely straightforward.

## The Wet Mattress: A Flawed Innovation

Desperate times lead to desperate measures. To battle the heat, some growers devised a low-cost greenhouse cooling system known informally as "the wet mattress."

This was no luxury device. It was a makeshift contraption: a porous fabric—often resembling a thick, felt mattress—was hung on one wall of the greenhouse. A water hose dripped water down its surface while an industrial fan blew air across it, hoping to cool the air through evaporation.

The intentions were noble; the results, disastrous. The added humidity created a perfect breeding ground for botrytis, and at a time when water was already unaffordable, this cooling system guzzled even more of it. The "wet mattress" didn't just fail to save the flowers—it actively contributed to their decay and cost growers thousands in wasted inventory and water bills.

## The Financial Fallout

The combination of worker exploitation scandals, climate instability, product degradation, flawed greenhouse innovation, and skyrocketing claims created a business environment that felt like quicksand. Every week, we were shipping goods that might come back to haunt us in the form of losses and damaged relationships.

*Learned Lesson: Interconnectedness and the Unforeseen Consequences of Solutions*

*In complex systems, every fix has a ripple effect. Solving one issue—like cooling the greenhouse—can inadvertently amplify others, like mold and cost overruns. Real solutions require holistic thinking. Understand how labor conditions, water access, plant biology, and logistics all intertwine. Don't isolate problems. Map the entire ecosystem.*

Reflection and Wrap-up:

This was our reality at the end of 2005. The system was showing cracks in every direction. And while most would've doubled down on damage control, I saw something else: an opportunity to reimagine the entire supply chain. The next chapter would take me far from Israel—to a continent that, at the time, few in the flower industry had dared to bet on.

# Chapter 11:

# The African Horizon Beckons

## A Seed of Opportunity in the Eye of the Storm

It was early February 2006, and I still remember the soft, steady rain falling over Israel that morning. My "office" at the time was usually the company car—I was almost always on the move, crisscrossing the country, meeting with flower growers, negotiating, learning, and troubleshooting. But something was brewing inside me. That day, I sat at a physical desk with a keyboard and monitor, driven by a question I could no longer ignore.

I approached one of the company's co-founders with a deceptively simple inquiry: *"Why are we only exporting flowers from Israel? Why aren't we sourcing from other countries?"*

Technically, we had some international export— passive ones. Some non-English-speaking clients would ask us to place routine standing orders with farms in Ecuador, and we'd arrange for deliveries to Holland. But our role was bureaucratic: send an email, confirm a date, add a small commission per stem, and done. We weren't curating or expanding anything. We were middlemen.

To my surprise, the company owner didn't dismiss the idea. He said, "Great idea. Find something." Then he handed me two thick brochures from a past international flower expo—mostly featuring growers from Ecuador, Colombia, and the Netherlands, with a few from Ethiopia. Was this a mandate? Not officially. But I took it as one. It was enough.

I had already imported tech products from China using Alibaba.com, so I knew how to navigate international sourcing. The next morning, I launched a deep online research session, determined to map global flower-growing markets.

My digital exploration, however, was cut short. When the company owner walked in and saw me immersed in online research, he snapped. "Stop wasting time. Get back in the field and find new growers here in Israel." That directive could've been a dead end. But I had two advantages: I had a track record of delivering results, and I didn't give up easily.

Instead of arguing, I got into the car and hit the road, scouting local growers as requested. But after hours—often late into the night—I continued my global search from home. I tapped into every skill I'd built from importing and negotiating in my previous ventures. Within a few weeks, I had narrowed my focus to two potential sources: Ethiopia and Kenya.

Ethiopia didn't pan out. The timing and infrastructure just weren't right. But Kenya? Kenya looked promising.

I began engaging with multiple Kenyan growers—vetting them through Alibaba and the now-ancient MSN Messenger. Thanks to my security and trade background, I could quickly separate the scammers from the serious. Through this vetting process, I discovered one particular farm that stood out. Over the next few years, I would help transform that farm into a leading player in the global flower trade.

## Old-School vs. Field-Driven Strategy

My approach clashed with management. They wanted me to work from directories, call growers first, and only visit in person if necessary. But I believed in personal contact. That belief wasn't theoretical—it was forged years earlier, when I was just 14.

Back then, I was knocking on doors, selling paintings. I developed three core skills:

1. **Foot in the Door:** If I could get my foot into someone's home, I had a 50% chance of making a sale.

2. **Empathy and Connection:** My aim was to open dialogue. I wasn't there to pressure anyone—I was there to read the room, build rapport, and let connection drive the sale.

3. **Big Object, Big Disruption:** Many of my prospects were glued to the TV watching sports. So, I'd place the largest painting I carried right in front of their screen. It startled them. It created a break in their routine—and opened a window for conversation and persuasion.

These weren't just sales tactics. They were early lessons in human behavior, communication, and resilience. And they stuck with me. It's why I believed a face-to-face meeting over coffee was more valuable than 10 phone calls. It's why I used the company car—or my own—to make those connections in person.

Eventually, those results were undeniable. The company gave me full rein over our flower business. I didn't ask for control. I earned it by delivering results that couldn't be ignored.

### Learned Lesson: Drive, Adaptability, and the Power of Personal Connection

*Real initiative doesn't always come with clear permission. Sometimes you have to move forward in the gray zone, trusting your vision and backing it up with effort. When others don't believe in your idea, believe enough in yourself—and do the work after hours if you must. Technology opens doors, but human connection cements relationships. A strong handshake, a shared coffee, and an honest conversation can outperform any digital tool* when it comes to building trust. Combine relentless drive with emotional intelligence, and you can turn even the smallest spark into a global breakthrough.

# Chapter 12:

# Elizabeth and the African Ascent

## The Unsung Hero and a Collision of Worlds

To truly play on the global stage, you need more than ambition—you need to decode the systems, cultures, and quiet signals that shape markets. This chapter opens the curtain on a world few ever see.

Her name was Elizabeth—a calm, brilliant Kenyan woman who answered my exploratory call with grace and clarity. She was working at one of the flower companies I'd uncovered during my research, and from the moment she picked up, I knew I wasn't just speaking to a receptionist. I was speaking to someone who could become the quiet cornerstone of something much bigger.

Elizabeth didn't just provide basic answers. She offered context, nuance, and insights that most gatekeepers wouldn't have thought to share. She incredibly nice, remarkably sharp, and unfailingly composed. And although she remained relatively anonymous to the outside world, her contribution to the massive cross-border trade project I was about to build was foundational. I say this without exaggeration: Elizabeth should be known, acknowledged, and celebrated.

At the time, Kenya's flower exports primarily flowed into the illustrious Aalsmeer Flower Auction in the Netherlands. Their largest buyers were European supermarkets—demanding consistency, reliability, and a narrow profile of product: short-stemmed, tightly closed flowers that would open over time, maximizing shelf life.

Most of the farms in Kenya could meet these exacting standards, and I would later come to work with nearly all of them, guiding them to scale up their production and improve profitability.

Elizabeth and I were an unlikely pairing. My style was relentless: fast-moving, highly detail-oriented, and often impatient with inefficiency. In contrast, Kenyan business culture—particularly at the time—flowed with a rhythm of "Hakuna Matata," a philosophy of "no worries" that often translated to missed deadlines, vague updates, and practices that I found hard to digest. I was shocked to discover things like trucks rerouted mid-journey so the driver could sell flowers to a competitor, or boxes packed half-empty to save time. Mistakes weren't just common—they were expected. I demanded a different level of performance: 30% reliability to start, but a target of 80% and beyond. It would take time, trust, and a whole lot of persistence to even get close.

But back to Elizabeth.

From her, I obtained my first real sense of the opportunity. She described four separate farms, including one in Arusha, Tanzania, each operating at different altitudes, producing distinct varieties of flowers. She also sent me their comprehensive price list. More than just numbers, it was an open invitation into their world—a window into the mechanics of supply.

One crucial detail Elizabeth shared changed everything: the company worked with an Israeli agricultural advisor, funded by an international bank. That connection mattered. It validated their credibility and added a layer of technical trust that I couldn't ignore. I contacted the advisor directly. That conversation helped me understand their internal operations and reassured me that I wasn't diving into a black box.

But logistics—that was the real monster.

The existing system in Kenya was simple. Flowers moved from farm to Nairobi's Jomo Kenyatta International Airport (JKIA), flew to the Netherlands, and were delivered straight to auction. The process took in average, 48 hours, give or take. My vision? Flowers from Kenya—or even cross-border from Tanzania—delivered not to Europe, but to Russia. And not just to Moscow. To the outer regions, where infrastructure was patchy and transit times could stretch beyond five days. It wasn't just a long supply chain—it was a high-risk, perishable, logistics puzzle, where every mistake could mean losses.

But if you've read this far, you know I'm not easily deterred.

That first call with Elizabeth laid the groundwork. She had no idea her role was about to grow dramatically. But she didn't flinch. She handled the growing complexity, the increasing demands, and the constant pressure with a steadiness that anchored the entire early-stage operation.

She wasn't a C-level executive. She didn't have a fancy title. But she had something more important: knowledge, integrity, and follow-through. And in frontier markets, where systems don't always work the way they should, those qualities are gold.

### Learned Lesson: The Unseen Champions and the Gap in Execution

*Never overlook the people behind the curtain. Visionaries may lead, but it's the Elizabeths of the world who turn ideas into action. They hold the keys to data, process, and execution. And they rarely get the spotlight.*

*Also, culture matters. Operational discipline looks different in different places. Success means bridging those cultural divides and translating bold ideas into workable, efficient systems. Global growth isn't just about having a good idea. It's about understanding the entire chain—people, process, culture, and timing—and building trust at every step.*

Reflection and Wrap-up:

The power in any product lies not just in how it's made, but in how deeply you understand who it's for—and why. Cultural context is often your sharpest competitive edge. What you know matters. But how well you know your customer and / or supplier—and the unspoken patterns of their world—matters more. Study culture as closely as you study product. That's where the margins are hiding.

# Chapter 13:

# The Audacity of the Outsider

## Building Bridges from a Humble Desk in Israel

To succeed at the highest levels in business, especially in new markets, you must be willing to operate outside your job title—and often, outside your comfort zone.

Back in Israel, I was still officially just a field operator. My access to company clients was practically nonexistent. Most of what I learned came from listening—overhearing the sales manager's conversations, catching details in passing, and quietly piecing things together. But I wasn't content to stay in the margins. I had a vision.

With a combination of persistence and the same scrappy mindset that had carried me since my teen years, I secured contact details for a few key clients. I introduced myself confidently, if humbly. It wasn't flashy—I was simply a guy with a new product and a new country of origin. But I knew how to open doors. My first entry in came thanks to a client who agreed to look at flowers from Kenya. That "yes" was everything. He'd try them out. No payment, just a willingness to evaluate.

That was my break.

I had now assembled a credible value chain: a serious supplier (thanks to Elizabeth), a solid price list, diverse varieties, and a curious buyer willing to test our offer. I walked into the company owner's office not just with ideas—but with a functioning prototype of a new business model. This wasn't just research anymore. It was real.

I'll spare you the minute-by-minute account of the grueling weeks that followed—the paperwork, the failures, the missed calls, the tightrope of internal politics and external logistics. Instead, let's jump ahead to the moment that changed everything: I booked my first flight to Kenya in early 2006.

Everyone else at the company remained locked into their routines, sending emails and reordering known goods from known suppliers. I, on the other hand, was heading to a new continent, building a new supply chain, and preparing to launch a new era in our trade strategy. It was the kind of bold, seemingly irrational move that transforms a footnote employee into a leader.

*Learned Lesson: Proactive Initiative and Leveraging Small Wins*

*Big shifts start small. A supplier's phone number. A single product sample. A client willing to try. These are the bricks. The mortar is **initiative**—the drive to connect the dots before anyone asks you to. You don't need full permission to lead. Just proof that you can.*

Reflection and Wrap-up:

Sometimes, what moves the needle isn't your position—it's your posture. If you act like an owner and build like a founder, others eventually follow your lead. Don't wait to be promoted before you think like a founder. When you show results, roles adjust around you. Let your impact speak louder than your job title.

# Chapter 14:
# Africa: A Love Affair Begins

## Navigating the Unknown with Instinct and Audacity

Africa: a continent that, for me, became an instant, profound love affair from the very first day. Stepping off that plane, my English was, to be frank, very basic—a real hurdle in meeting Elizabeth and the owner of the flower group she worked for. But what I lacked in language, I made up for in something just as powerful: body language. Years in security and the chaos of nightclub ownership had sharpened my ability to read people, to communicate with subtlety and conviction without saying a word.

I also knew virtually nothing about Kenya—its culture, norms, geography, or infrastructure. But that blank slate was a gift. It made me humble. It made me observant. And it made me open to absorbing everything around me without assumptions.

Friends from my security days had jokingly warned me to bring a private military helicopter armed with advanced surveillance equipment and ammunition. The idea was laughable. But strangely, it stuck. Their exaggeration carried a seed of truth: when entering unfamiliar terrain, awareness and caution are essential. That mindset served me well.

The owner of the Subati Group—a gentleman I remember as Mr. Combos—made good on his word. A driver picked me up from the airport. I was grateful, but my instincts kicked in immediately. Before we even left the parking lot, I insisted the driver lock all doors and roll up the windows. It wasn't just nerves; it was muscle memory. Back home, I hated the heat. But here, despite the summer sun, I needed the sense of safety. Driving through Nairobi, it felt like my security friends were whispering in my ear again. Nearly every building was surrounded by electric fences and guarded gates. There were few expats. No luxury storefronts. It was raw. It was real.

The next morning, at precisely 5:00 AM, I was expected to be ready for a long drive to Subukia—home of the Subati group of farms. We passed Lake Nanyuki, crossed the equator, and entered a mountainous region that seemed untouched by time. That journey changed me.

And then, I tasted Chapati and Sukuma Wiki for the first time.

It might sound like a small detail, but I remember it vividly. Sukuma Wiki—Swahili for "push the week"—was more than a dish. It was a symbol. A staple for families, it was hearty, comforting, and made with collard greens stewed in tomato, onion, and spice. Served with warm, chewy Chapati, it tasted like resilience. Like home, even though I was thousands of miles from mine.

Those early days weren't easy. The formality of meetings, the cultural dance of communication, the isolation—it could've easily broken someone less committed. But instead, something unexpected happened: I fell in love. With the landscape. With the challenge. And with the people.

This wasn't just a business trip anymore. It was the beginning of a partnership. A trust-building exercise. A transformation.

### Learned Lesson: Embrace the Unfamiliar and Trust Your Instincts

*You don't need fluency to connect. You don't need a playbook to lead. When you show up with respect, curiosity, and presence, you earn trust. And when you combine sharp instincts with deep listening, even a foreign land can become a second home.*

### Reflection and Wrap-up:

**True growth begins where comfort ends. When you step into the unknown with humility and instinct, you expand not just your business—but more importantly your worldview.**

**Don't let unfamiliarity scare you away. Let it sharpen your**

edge. New markets—and new relationships—often begin with nothing more than a handshake, a shared meal, and the courage to keep showing up.

# Chapter 15:
# The Great Rift Valley and the Business of Blooms

## Of Epic Landscapes and Market Demands

I was informed that, due to the challenging road conditions—or, to be more precise, the sheer lack of proper roads for at least half the journey—our trip to Subati farm might take a staggering five to six hours one way. This wasn't merely a commute; it was an expedition.

I would divide my transformative trip into two distinct sections. The first involved driving from Nairobi to Naivasha. After we left the bustling city area and passed what locals simply referred to as "The Wall" (a significant landmark I will circle back to later, as it holds its own story), we suddenly entered the awe-inspiring Great Rift Valley. It is a colossal land depression, a geological marvel formed approximately 20 million years ago, plunging to depths of 2,000 meters in some places. It is a breathtaking expanse, dotted with ancient lakes and dormant volcanoes, a colossal geological scar that stretches across the entire African continent, reaching north towards Egypt and almost extending up to Israel. I distinctly remember on one of my subsequent trips to Kenya, while visiting another flower farm in Eldoret town, passing a billboard that starkly declared: "**From Here To Jerusalem 9600 km.**" It was a powerful reminder of the vast distances and profound connections across this ancient land.

The second part of the journey, at least for me, truly began from Nakuru town. Back in 2006, Nakuru itself was already a significant three-and-a-half to four-hour drive from Nairobi. From Nakuru, we began a slow, winding climb into the majestic mountains, and it was precisely here that I unequivocally fell in love with Kenya. The landscape transformed into breathtaking beauty: rolling mountains crowned with the iconic acacia trees, just like those I'd seen in countless books and movies, their distinctive silhouettes etched against the sky. Everywhere, there were vibrant flower farms and rich coffee plantations, many of them surprisingly cultivated in open fields rather than protected greenhouses, a testament to the ideal climate. Who could have known back then that I would find my spiritual and professional home in this very place for the next 12 years of my life? For those who are interested in the deeper geographical and cultural wonders of Kenya, I would heartily refer you to National Geographic, my book, fundamentally, is about business, strategic thinking, and the relentless spirit of entrepreneurship.

To consistently make money in this demanding industry, you must build a business based on a product whose success is directly related to the precise number of flowers your potential client needs, and whose market demand is intrinsically regulated by the fluctuating human emotions of happiness or sorrow. Both emotions, incidentally, equally impact demand, though they call for different types of flowers in each occasion. The challenge, and the genius, lay in navigating this emotional economy with precise logistical and product-specific solutions.

### *Learned Lesson: Connecting Market Needs to Emotional Drivers*

*Sustainable business success often comes from identifying and directly connecting your product or service to fundamental human needs and emotional drivers, whether they are celebrations of happiness or expressions of sorrow. Beyond raw quantity, understand the why behind demand. Furthermore, recognize that your journey will take you to unexpected places, geographically and personally. Embrace the beauty and challenges of new environments, as they can reveal not only untapped business opportunities but als a deeper understanding of yourself and the world.*

### Reflection and Wrap-up:

**Success often lies in forging emotional resonance with your product. Understanding geography, culture, and**

client emotion turns an ordinary business into an extraordinary one. What you sell matters. But why people buy it—and how it fits into the rhythm of their lives— matters even more. Follow emotion. Follow the land. That's where your market lives.

# Chapter 16:
# The Promise of Kenya

Unearthing Opportunity in an Unexpected Landscape

I can't recall the exact size of the old Subati farm, but I vividly remember its rose varieties – a modest fourteen or sixteen different types, a stark contrast to the diverse spectrum I would later manage. Upon arriving at the farm, I was introduced to the farm manager, an elderly British gentleman whose name, regrettably, escapes me now. As we walked through the surprisingly beautiful greenhouses – a stark, inspiring contrast to the partially abandoned, broken, and poorly maintained structures I'd grown accustomed to in Israel, a grim testament to high operational costs – two critical observations immediately seized my attention. First, most of the flowers were harvested with tightly closed, small heads. Second, and far more excitingly, these flowers possessed an incredible inherent strength, exceptional quality, and unbelievably vibrant colors, especially when compared to the very same varieties we struggled to grow in Israel. To put it simply, I saw a huge, untapped opportunity.

The Kenyan fresh-cut flower industry, at that moment, was absolutely unprepared for the demands of our target markets and the transformative changes I was about to implement. Farmers were primarily focused on sending hundreds of boxes of uniform flowers directly to the Aalsmeer auction in Holland, adhering to a conventional model. No one was considering mixing varieties within shipments, consolidating different flowers from the same farm, let alone strategically consolidating diverse flowers from across the entire country to meet specific, high-demand market niches. *It was a factory mindset, not a market-driven one.*

Promising the prospect of massive future sales volumes, I managed to convince Elizabeth and Mr. Combos that I urgently needed samples and a little bit of time to prove the concept. The good thing, as I've mentioned before, is that time in Kenya often flows differently; everything moves at a deliberately slow pace, if it moves at all. Over my seventeen years of working with and within Kenya, I honed my skills, learning to effortlessly navigate most uncertainties and later, advise countless startups and investors from diverse fields on how to thrive in such environments. This foundational experience in Kenya ultimately became a cornerstone of my expertise as an advisor.

After returning from the Subati farm, I visited two more farms within the Nairobi area, opting to skip for this initial trip, the Hortanzia farm located much further afield in Arusha, Tanzania. I personally and meticulously chose the specific varieties that I believed our Russian and former USSR clients would be most eager to see, relying heavily on the knowledge I had gained tirelessly running around Israel, searching for farmers and understanding their rose output. In the next few days, I was genuinely surprised when the farms, using their own delivery trucks that normally transported flowers to the airport, began dropping off these crucial sample flowers directly at the Subati Group office.

Fresh-cut flowers, ideally, should be maintained at a consistent temperature of 4 degrees Celsius (about 38°F) all the way from harvest to their final destination to preserve their delicate beauty and extend their vase life. Yet, these samples arrived at the office in trucks that, despite assurances, lacked any refrigerated sections. To compound the problem, a few bunches of flowers that had been forgotten at one of the farms were sent to the office by taxi— a vehicle that, predictably, did not use its air conditioning system. I put "reduce fuel consumption" in brackets intentionally here, because the reality was that any perceived "fuel reduction" had nothing to do with genuine company savings; it was often about drivers skimming fuel money, using the balance for lunch for themselves, or sometimes even for an entire team or department. Some might try to accuse me of bias, but I urge you not to, unless you have lived in Kenya for as long as I have and possess deep security and risk assessment knowledge of such operational realities.

Consequently, it took almost two full days to gather all the sample flowers at the office, where they were kept in simple buckets in a kitchen—a logistical nightmare for highly perishable goods. Just for clarification, keeping flowers—especially roses—in Israel without proper cold storage conditions would lead to their death before shipment. To be honest, the majority of our Israeli roses were already in such poor condition even with maintaining regulations; this was precisely the reason I embarked on this whole project to find better sources.

Okay, so now all the samples were finally gathered. Elizabeth, with her calm competence, promised to organize the shipment and all necessary documentation according to our specific needs. The flowers were to be delivered to our handling company in Holland, the same trusted partner we used for all our existing flower shipments to our clients. This marked the end of my first visit to Kenya. I returned to Israel, brimming with information, and delivered a detailed report to our company owner and other managers, a report that likely sounded more like an audacious proposal than a standard update.

### Learned Lesson: The Power of Contrast and Unseen Challenges

*True opportunity often reveals itself in stark contrast to existing limitations. Don't just look for improvement; seek out what is fundamentally different and potentially transformative, even if it comes with its own set of hidden, frustrating challenges (like temperature control in a "non-refrigerated" truck). Embrace the grit of the field, for it exposes realities that no office report ever could. Understanding and navigating these "unseen" operational realities, including cultural quirks and local practices, is as crucial as identifying the initial market opportunity.*

## Reflection and Wrap-up:

**Real breakthroughs happen when you're willing to step into logistical chaos, listen beyond what's being said, and trust what your instincts see in contrast. A business isn't just about margins or efficiency—it's about vision that sees potential where others see problems. Your edge is not just in spotting opportunities, but in navigating the chaos required to bring them to life.**

# Chapter 17:
# The Test of Fire

## From Scepticism to a Game-Changing Call

After the logistical nightmare of simply bringing the samples from the farms to Mr. Combos' offices in Kenya, I honestly didn't harbor grand expectations for that trial shipment. I was almost certain the flowers wouldn't survive even the flight to Holland. The process was fraught with peril: after our handling company collected those few boxes (a mere 500 stems in total) from the airline in Holland, they were then supposed to add these boxes to a designated truck company that would drive all the way from Holland in Europe to Moscow, Russia. There, our main client would receive these boxes and then distribute them onward to their final destinations—the end clients who had bravely agreed to "look at these flowers." This entire journey for a highly sensitive, short-vase-life product was projected to take an agonizing eight to nine days, a stark contrast to the maximum of two days for shipments from Israel (assuming no flight delays or offloaded boxes due to lack of aircraft space). The odds were stacked against us.

Ten agonizing days after the samples were harvested, our client in Moscow finally received the boxes. His immediate feedback, sent in a series of very disappointing pictures, showed totally damaged boxes, with some flowers hanging despondently outside of the packaging. My heart sank. I was informed that he would "treat them" and "put them on water"—a critical term in the flower industry. This process involves carefully removing the flowers from their boxes, recutting their stems at an angle, and then placing them in water, often with a special hydrating solution, in a cold room. The goal is to "wake up" the flowers, allowing them to drink enough water and regain their strength, preparing them to be sold. We had four more days to wait for his next report.

After those additional four days, counting back, it meant it had now been an astonishing sixteen to eighteen days since those flowers were first harvested from the farms in Kenya. Then, the call came. The client called our office and specifically asked to speak with me directly. My stomach clenched. The only thing Gocha, my client, said, with an almost incredulous tone, was: *"Yuly, I want one more trial shipment, for free."*

Without a moment's hesitation, without even contemplating asking our company owner for permission, I gave him my immediate answer by asking: "When?" My entrepreneurial mindset, a finely tuned instrument of opportunity detection, told me that even if the company owner ultimately refused to cover the cost, I would personally pay for that shipment myself. From the deep impression of what I had seen in Kenya – the sheer resilience and vibrant quality of their flowers, even after such rough handling – and the utterly unexpected response from our client, I intuitively saw a huge opportunity and undeniable potential for success. This was the validation I needed.

For the next few months, our shipments—our trial orders—started to grow, slowly but steadily. Yet, it was still a very small operation, not yet substantial enough to be called a "business" in any grand sense. We were shipping up to 3,000 stems per month, painstakingly and slowly increasing the number of clients who were willing to accept a trial shipment and crucially, later committed to buying the flowers regularly.

At the same time, I started feeling a palpable sense of frustration and tension emanating from our company manager, my direct boss, who traditionally handled the Israeli flower supply. He clearly saw that I was moving fast and growing into new territory, while he seemed stuck, managing the same old problems of the past. I began communicating more frequently with Elizabeth, building an even stronger rapport. While I was still dutifully driving around Israel, performing my original field duties, I also became increasingly involved in domestic operational tasks. I already knew the Israeli growers intimately, I had forged relationships with the airfreight agents at the airport while helping our drivers offload flowers late at night at Ben Gurion Airport, and because Kenya's shipments were still relatively small, I found myself more deeply involved in communicating directly with our clients. I was building new price lists specifically for Kenyan roses, and crucially, advising our Israeli sales manager on how we could attract new clients by strategically balancing the commission structures between Israeli and Kenyan flowers. This was essential because competition among all exporters in Israel was incredibly tight, leaving very little room for price negotiations.

I knew that shipping a mere 3,000 stems per month was not an interesting or scalable business model. Something bigger had to be done. My sights turned to the largest international flower expo, held annually in Moscow, usually around September. This was one of the three main global flower expos, alongside the biggest one in Holland and another in Ecuador. I had a clear, audacious plan forming in my head for achieving significant results.

During this transformative period, I managed to visit Kenya one or two more times, each trip further solidifying orders and sales, and deepening my relationships with the farm managers and of course, Elizabeth. My relentless drive and the tangible results I was producing propelled me rapidly within our company. I was first promoted to Manager, and then very quickly advanced to the position of General Manager of the Export Fresh Cut Flowers business. The scale of my influence was dramatically expanding.

In this pivotal year of 2006, I made sure to visit both the Moscow Flower Expo and the expo in Holland, seizing the opportunity to visit the legendary Aalsmeer Flower Auction itself. Since my parents had taken me from Moscow in 1990 to move to Israel, I had only returned once, briefly, in 2002 for a few days. Visiting the flower expo marked only my second time back in Russia. I informed our company owner that I needed to go early and stay longer after the expo—a request that, once again, did not make him particularly happy. But slowly, he was beginning to listen to my increasingly data-driven opinions. This was the only year where I did not take part in preparing our company's representative booth at the expo; my mission was far more strategic.

In Moscow, I visited almost every single big and middle-range company that imported flowers. Even more importantly, I spent a significant amount of time visiting individual florist shops—which are massive in number across Russia, given how integral flowers are to the culture! I learned an immense amount from this visit, insights so numerous and profound that there will simply not be enough space in this book to list everything. But there are a few crucial points I want to highlight, and I will start with the most impactful conclusion.

*Learned Lesson: The Power of Unexpected Validation and Calculated Risk*

*Don't let initial failures or logistical setbacks define your potential. The most valuable validation often comes from unexpected places and in surprising forms. Be willing to take calculated personal risks (like paying for a trial shipment yourself) when your gut tells you an opportunity is immense. True entrepreneurial vision recognizes the "win" even in a seemingly "damaged" product if the underlying quality and market demand are there. Furthermore, consistent, albeit small, wins build credibility and momentum, allowing you to gradually overcome internal resistance and expand your influence.*

**Reflection and Wrap-up:**

**Big opportunities often come dressed as damaged goods. If you're paying attention, even setbacks can whisper potential.**
**You don't need to have full control to spark change—you just need enough proof, passion, and courage to make your case undeniable. Every crack in the wall is a chance to build your door.**

# Chapter 18:
# The End-User Revelation
## The Hidden Truths from the Front Lines of Flower Sales

In 2024, I watched a video featuring Aaron Spivak, the founder of Hush, who started his company with just $4,000 and grew it into a multi-million-dollar brand. He shared his "secret" to success—and it was shockingly simple. They continuously engaged with their customers, asking how they imagined the product, what would make them buy, and what real-life problem it would solve. In business-speak, they mastered the Customer Profile and Value Map.

But nearly two decades earlier, in 2006, I was doing exactly that—instinctively.

Back then, during one of my visits to Moscow, I didn't limit myself to feedback from importers and wholesalers. I went straight to the front lines: over 50 florist shops of all sizes, from sprawling storefronts to tiny sidewalk tables under the open sky. I asked real questions of real sellers: *"What problems do you have with the flowers you're receiving? What's missing? What varieties do you wish were in your cold room right now?"*

It wasn't a one-time research blitz. This was an active process I kept up for over a decade, until 2017, when I eventually closed my own flower export business in Kenya. And I want you to pause and absorb this: if you're building a business, or selling anything at all, this principle is a game changer.

Don't just talk to your direct clients. Importers and wholesalers are important, sure—but their view is filtered. They often don't understand what the flower shop really needs. And they're not motivated to find out. Their model is bulk, logistics, margins. Not end-user joy.

The true insights—the gold—come from the florists who speak to end buyers every day. Some of the best revelations I received were from shopkeepers working in crumbling sheds with handwritten price tags and tired refrigerators. But they knew. They told me what varieties consistently sold out. What colors were trending. What bouquets were rejected.

My competitors didn't go that deep. Which meant they didn't see what I saw.

### Learned Lesson: Go Directly to the End-User

*Never rely solely on feedback from intermediaries in your supply chain. The most profound insights and game-changing solutions for your business reside with the ultimate end-user or the final point of sale. Engage with those who actually use or interact with your product. Their unfiltered frustrations and specific desires will provide the real "customer profile and value map" that can differentiate your business, drive innovation, and unlock exponential growth. The truth—and your biggest opportunity—is often found on the street, not in the boardroom.*

## Reflection and Wrap-up:

Big data matters. But small talk—the kind that happens in cramped flower shops and roadside stalls—is often the source of your biggest breakthroughs.The closer you get to the person who makes the final decision—the buyer, the user, the one holding the wallet or the heart—the clearer your path to success becomes. Listen harder. Dig deeper. That's where the real edge lives.

# Chapter 19:
# Whispers from the Moscow Streets
## Unmasking the Reality of the Flower Trade

Here's what I learned, and some of the critical pain points I unearthed, directly from the front lines of Moscow's flower market. The insights were staggering, revealing a profound disconnect between suppliers and their ultimate customers.

The majority of florists and salespeople working in those countless shops simply did not know that the flowers were imported. They genuinely believed that the vibrant flowers gracing their displays were grown locally, somewhere just beyond the city limits. In some rare cases, they knew—or perhaps merely believed—that certain flowers originated from Colombia, Ecuador, a small percentage from Israel, and the rest were magically grown in Holland. But these informed individuals were a tiny minority, lost amidst a vast sea of unawareness.

Perhaps even more critically, almost all of the Russians working in or owning these flower businesses did not speak English. Furthermore, many of them were not technologically advanced; using an online translator for them was as complex and intimidating as being asked to pilot a jet airplane. This communication barrier meant that essential feedback and real-time market needs were simply not reaching the exporters.

Compounding this was a deep-seated, largely negative perception of Kenya ingrained from childhood. The USSR, and later Russia, instilled a perception of Africa that was mostly negative, shaped by outdated books. I distinctly remember the story by Kornei Chukovsky's *Barmaley* (1925), which painted a dark Africa—wild, foreboding, a place to be avoided, populated mostly by gorillas, crocodiles, and terrifying monsters. Asking these florists if they had ever seen flowers from Kenya often elicited a very negative, almost disgusted, reaction. The brand image of Kenya as a flower source was non-existent or actively detrimental.

Their practical complaints were consistent and damning: many imported flowers had a short vase life and small heads. The unanimous consensus was that only roses from Ecuador and Colombia were truly suitable for the demanding Russian market—flowers with robust, big heads and impressive stems ranging from 60 cm to a majestic 100 cm tall.

Finally, they universally complained about poor packaging. Shipments often arrived with a significant number of damaged and broken stems, leading to substantial losses for their businesses. Did you ever ask yourself why flowers cost so much in a shop? Well, now you know: the inherent fragility, the complex supply chain, and these avoidable damages all contribute to the exorbitant price tag that the end consumer ultimately bears.

These were the pain points, raw and unfiltered, that revealed the true market opportunity.

### Learned Lesson: The Value of Unfiltered End-User Feedback

*Never assume your market's understanding of your product or its origin. Go directly to the final point of sale to uncover fundamental misconceptions and critical pain points. Overcome language and cultural barriers to access honest, unfiltered feedback, as this ground-level intelligence is invaluable. The highest margins are often found in addressing the seemingly minor frustrations of your last-mile customers—especially those related to quality, consistency, and packaging, as these directly impact their profitability and perceived value.*

### Reflection and Wrap-up:

**Behind every complaint is a roadmap. Listen to the right people, and you'll hear what the market truly wants. Don't try to correct the market from afar. Meet it where it lives—on the street, in the shop, at the hands of the florist**

who has five seconds to decide whether to reorder or never buy from you again.

# Chapter 20:
# Magic, Confusion, and the Russian Soul

## Navigating Holidays, Logistics, and Cultural Nuances

The year 2007 felt like being inside a cyclone. At just 29, I had stepped fully into the role of General Manager, and the pressure was unrelenting. I was driving forward our newly developing Kenya operations while still neck-deep in the established Israeli flower export business. Days blurred together as I pushed Elizabeth and her Kenyan team—hard. We worked tirelessly to boost quality, expand volume, and prepare for what would be my biggest test yet: Russia's national flower holidays.

If you've never sold flowers in Russia, let me explain something critical. It's not just about Valentine's Day or birthdays. The Russian calendar is lined with flower-centric cultural events, deeply rooted in Soviet tradition and still alive today. The most powerful of them all? International Women's Day on March 8th. Others include the Last Day of School and the First Day of School (September 1st), both national rituals involving kids giving flowers to their teachers. May 9th—Victory Day—is another big one, along with Tatyana's Day and many other commemorative occasions.

Back then, Valentine's Day wasn't a massive commercial holiday in Russia yet, which worked in our favor. After the Kenyan farms met Europe's Valentine's demand, we could redirect capacity toward Russia's massive Women's Day spike. I didn't yet understand how deep the rabbit hole went in terms of harvest cycles and planting schedules—but I was about to learn through experience.

To grasp the full logistical dance, let's reverse-engineer the timeline:

- March 8: Men buy flowers.

- March 4: Florists need those flowers ready, hydrated, and "on water"—a term for letting them wake up after long travel.

- February 27: My wholesalers in Russia need to have them in stock, sorted and ready to distribute to the shops.

- February 20: The flowers must have already landed in Holland from Kenya, cleared customs, and been routed to Moscow.

- February 18: The latest date for the shipment to leave Kenya, meaning harvesting must start around February 16.

So, February 16—*that's* the real moment of truth.

Meanwhile, my Russian wholesalers were finalizing their orders by December 10 of the previous year. Some made small tweaks in January, but usually only to increase volumes. Orders were seven to twelve times higher than regular months. It was their version of Black Friday—except with roses instead of TV's. One client joked that after March 8, he could take the next three months off.

Now imagine Elizabeth's shock when, on December 15, I sent her an order ten times larger than anything we'd done before—and asked her to ship it in the middle of February.

She thought I was joking.

But what she didn't know was that I had reverse-engineered the entire demand cycle. I wasn't reacting—I was leading. While other suppliers jacked up prices, we kept ours flat. While others missed shipments, we delivered early. The result? We won over wholesalers who had been loyal to our competitors for years.

This was the "magic and confusion" of the Russian flower market. Magic in the margins. Confusion in the cultural rhythms. But once I decoded it—once I respected the entire choreography—I could dance circles around my competitors.

*Learned Lesson: Strategic Timing and Exploiting Market Asymmetries*

*Mastering the calendar of your market's peak demand periods is crucial for maximizing revenue. Furthermore, look for market asymmetries—discrepancies in pricing, supply, or information that others miss. While your competitors are doubling prices, leveraging a stable, high-quality, and cost-effective supply, especially during peak season, creates immense competitive advantage and cements client loyalty. The "magic" often lies in seeing connections and opportunities that are invisible to those focused solely on traditional patterns.*

**Reflection and Wrap-up: Seeing the System Behind the Sale & Decode Before You Deliver.**

**In business, we're often trained to react to demand. But what if your edge lies not in speed, but in anticipation? What if understanding the cultural calendar of your buyer—down to the school holidays and romantic traditions—gives you the kind of foresight spreadsheets never could? Russia's flower economy wasn't just about blooms. It was a mirror reflecting desire, ritual, and identity. Once I stopped shipping flowers and started interpreting patterns, I didn't just fill orders—I shaped them.**

To win in high-pressure markets, you have to become fluent in the rhythms your competitors don't even notice. Your true advantage might not be better pricing or faster logistics—but deeper cultural literacy. When others see chaos, look closer. Magic often hides inside confusion. And the Russian soul? It doesn't speak through emails or spreadsheets. It speaks through rituals, romance, and timing. Learn that language, and you'll never run out of opportunity.

*Trust and exceptional customer care, coupled with genuine empathy, are, in my experience, the most important factors in sustainable business.*

# Chapter 21:
# The Unfair Advantage

## Beyond Price: Vase Life, Trust, and The "Save Each Flower" Mentality

This chapter will highlight how a deep understanding of the market from one side, and the capabilities of suppliers from the other, can forge extraordinary business and financial opportunities.

That year, 2007, marked my first time working with Kenya on a major holiday, and it was not only a game-changer but also a critically high-stakes endeavor. I knew that soon, within a year or two, market dynamics would shift, and I needed to guarantee sustained success by taking the next step, or even several simultaneous steps, in different directions. My long-term vision was paramount.

I want to return to the Russian flower industry, which, I am sure, is not fundamentally different from any other. Everyone wants to make money, but this depends not only on the classical forces of demand, supply, and price but also on a myriad of other factors that I categorize simply as Risks.

We know that Women's Day on March 8th is when a man goes, either before, during, or after his workday, to buy flowers for the women in his life—which, by the way, typically includes his mother and even grandmother, if she is still alive. But there are many uncertainties that can derail this perfectly planned sequence. For example, a truck company owner, tasked with delivering flowers from and through Europe to Russia, might refuse to pay—or, let's call it, offer a "gift" to—a customs representative. Such a refusal could instantly create a significant delay in crossing the border. The truck might simply get stuck for an "extra customs inspection," a "security check," or any other fabricated reason based on how "offended" the person who didn't receive their "holiday gift" might feel. This could delay the truck by a day or two, critically impacting the delivery of flowers to the final florist shop. In such a scenario, the end client could receive the flowers  after the actual Women's Day.

Would you buy a turkey meant for Thanksgiving after the actual Thanksgiving, or a Christmas tree past Christmas? Probably not. First, because you might not celebrate it twice, or even if you're having a "Friendsgiving," you likely would have already purchased your turkey from another source, from a supplier who was smart enough to get the turkeys to you on time. Of course, with a turkey, it's easier because it can be frozen, and its shelf life is much longer. This is starkly different from fresh-cut flowers, which you must sell within a few crucial days before they start losing petals and "dropping heads."

Most flowers supplied from Israel, Holland (even those grown in Holland), and even Ecuador, if they weren't sold by March 14th, typically represented a 90% total loss. The inherent fragility and short vase life meant they were economically worthless. But Kenya was profoundly different. Kenyan roses had an extraordinarily long vase life. We reached a point where, even in the worst year, when the economy was down and Women's Day sales hit a record low, my clients could still successfully sell my Kenyan roses up to March 30th! Just imagine the immense value this provided to their businesses: how much I increased their chances for revenue and dramatically decreased their losses. To summarize, flowers harvested around February 17th could still be worked with and sold by clients in the final market until March 30th. Of course, this extended sales period might have slightly affected my immediate sales and revenue as an exporter (as clients didn't need to restock as quickly), but a happy and satisfied client will always make you happier in the long term. Trust and exceptional customer care, coupled with genuine empathy, are, in my experience, the most important factors in sustainable business.

In the flower business, there are unwritten rules and gentlemen's agreements that govern long-term relationships:

1. **Loyalty for Support**: If you help your client fulfill their orders during a major holiday, providing good market prices and quality, they will be fiercely loyal and supportive of you throughout the rest of the year, until the next major holiday. This builds enduring partnerships.

2. **"Save Each Flower"**: In the fresh-cut flower industry (at least the old-fashioned one), we used to have a mantra: "Save each flower." This meant that almost every flower, regardless of its initial condition, could find a buyer or be repurposed. Florists in flower shops are masters of this art, meticulously cleaning and preparing flowers for clients. This includes removing (peeling) bad, old, or damaged outer petals, carefully trimming damaged leaves, and sometimes even shortening long stems if the top of the stem was damaged, making them suitable for smaller arrangements. I've seen florists sell just flower heads where the stem was completely broken very close to the head itself. People used to buy these, placing them in a water plate, allowing them to float beautifully like miniature boats. It's a very beautiful setting for a dining table or an entrance to a home. I've done it many times myself, using a tall clay pot with water

and a few stems of roses floating, placing it at my house entrance – *simple elegance from salvaged beauty.*

3. **Supporting Growers**: While the desire to make money is a normal business approach, capitalizing on holiday sales is a tremendous opportunity not only to increase revenue but also to reduce financial risk for the rest of the year. Growers typically increase their prices significantly for holiday sales, and we, as buyers, would push them down as much as possible. And trust me, we could push a lot. However, to ensure everyone remained happy and supportive, the limit and our "hunger" for lower prices had to be balanced. In that delicate equilibrium, the grower would then support you through the leaner periods of the year. At least, that's how it used to work, a true partnership. Finally, now everyone was happy. I secured orders from my clients early enough, which allowed me to reliably reserve flowers, lock in crucial airfreight space, and secure favorable prices. At the same time, I could easily increase the price for Kenyan flowers by two or three times for my clients (and it was still lower than comparable flowers from other countries!) without Elizabeth needing to increase her prices to me. This immense margin was

my "unfair advantage" and a testament to the value I had unlocked.

As you can see, when I made the strategic decision to invest in the Kenyan market, I saw the opportunity not solely in direct pricing but by meticulously considering all these interconnected factors: vase life, price point, availability based on different holidays in different markets and countries, the intricacies of the global supply chain, and even the overarching global political situation that might impact not only supply chain transit times but also entire economies, markets, and even shifts in consumer fashion.

When people ask me about what I do or what I did, I often struggle for a concise answer. I cannot simply say I was "Exporting Flowers," because exporting flowers sounds boring and generic, completely failing to capture the depth and complexity of my work. I am still looking for that perfect, single sentence to answer that question.

I was living the flower business from the inside out and the outside in: meticulously forecasting demands, constantly changing and building innovative strategies, relentlessly improving quality, and, perhaps most profoundly, creating thousands of jobs by advising and helping flower growers to expand their operations.

My work significantly impacted Kenya's market share, helping it grow from a mere 0.5% to nearly 50% in target markets, successfully competing head-to-head against established giants like Ecuador and Colombia. I effectively rebranded Kenya's floral industry, showcasing its unique beauty, unparalleled quality, and undeniable charm to a skeptical world. I improved logistics, reducing transportation costs by up to an astonishing 30%. Ultimately, I contributed directly to the exponential growth of Kenya's flower exports, from a modest 273 million USD in 2005 to a staggering 663 million USD in 2023, making it the sixth-largest export market globally. This wasn't just exporting flowers; it was transforming an industry and creating a legacy.

### Learned Lesson: The Multidimensional Value Proposition

*Don't just sell a product; sell a solution that addresses your client's deepest pain points and unlocks their own profitability. The "unfair advantage" comes not just from a lower price, but from a multidimensional value proposition that includes superior quality (like extended vase life), unparalleled reliability, strategic timing, and a deep understanding of your client's entire operational and emotional landscape. Long-term success is built on a foundation of mutual trust and creating win-win scenarios across your entire supply chain, from grower to final customer. This holistic approach is what truly transforms a simple trade into a global impact.*

Reflection and Wrap-up: From Commodity to Legacy & Advantage is Earned, Not Given

True innovation doesn't always mean inventing something new—it means seeing the same market everyone else sees, but unlocking new value others overlook. My unfair advantage wasn't just about logistics or price—it was about perspective. I wasn't just shipping flowers; I was reshaping an entire supply chain, rebalancing risk, and quietly building a reputation rooted in trust. In a commoditized world, competitive edges don't come from shortcuts. They come from insight, empathy, and execution. The real unfair advantage is earned by connecting the dots others miss—between markets, cultures, timelines, and people. That's how you stop being just another exporter—and start becoming indispensable.

# Chapter 22:

# The First Contract

## Beyond Brokerage: The Quest for Deeper Profit and Control

In this pivotal chapter, I'll reveal what truly motivated me to pursue, and ultimately close, my very first flower growing contract—a direct agreement with the farm, bypassing the traditional middleman role. This was an extraordinary, real-world lesson that every entrepreneur should internalize, regardless of their industry. It dissects the decision-making process, highlights the unforeseen gaps, and frankly, exposes some of the mistakes I made along the way.

It's time to unveil a crucial secret: typically, a middleman company (an exporter like the one I worked for) would make an average commission of just $0.03 per stem. When I launched the Kenya project, I immediately elevated that number to $0.07 per stem. But with this first direct growing agreement, I boldly pushed that commission to an astounding $0.25 per stem for the first three years! Yes, I can imagine some of my readers might not be entirely happy with such a revelation—it's a significant leap in margins that few in the industry achieved.

Up until this moment, the company I worked for had rigidly adhered to a strategy of being a mere middleman.

Their approach was simple: find growers who could grow fspecific types of flowers, meet certain quality standards, and provide them within a defined price range. The most significant factor, however, was trust. Trust that they would consistently support our clients' needs throughout the year. Trust that they would proactively communicate any changes in their fields—be it a devastating flower disease, an unexpected water supply shortage, or even manpower issues on their farms that could impact supply. This last part was, in reality, extremely critical, often overlooked, and deeply problematic in the Israeli context. Let me provide a few illustrative examples.

### Learned Lesson: The Power of Direct Relationships and Vertical Integration

*Don't settle for standard industry margins if you can create greater value. Moving beyond a mere "middleman" role to establish direct growing contracts dramatically increases profitability and control over your supply chain. This deeper integration allows you to influence quality, secure consistent supply, and build the kind of proactive trust with your suppliers that insulates you from common industry pitfalls. The more control you have over the source, the more power you have in the market.*

Reflection and Wrap-up:

This chapter wasn't just about securing higher margins—it was about stepping into ownership of my destiny. The move to direct contracting marked a moment where I stopped reacting to market conditions and started shaping them. For anyone seeking to grow in business, ask yourself: where are you still waiting on someone else to act? And what's one area where taking the driver's seat could change your outcomes forever?

# Chapter 23: The Israeli Grower's Dilemma

## Weather, Holidays, and the Boomerang of Trust

Growers in Israel operated under an unwritten law, largely a tradition dictated by the extreme weather conditions. Due to the intense heat, people on farms would work from very early morning up until noon, then retreat for a long siesta, resting or sleeping until 2 PM or even 4 PM. As an exporter, we were dependent on numerous factors, the most important being the availability of flight capacity and how quickly we could process flowers in a relatively hot environment. This wasn't limited to flowers that thrived in the heat, like some green fillers, but roses, in particular, struggled immensely. The heat negatively affected head size, stem length, and critically, accelerated the spread of diseases like botrytis, especially after a flower was harvested. The other persistent problem of hot weather was the challenge of storing flowers and their transportation, a point I will delve into in a later chapter.

*A quick note on terms: A Green Filler is a plant, often foliage or delicate flower or a small tree branch, that can be used along side flowers to make a bouquet or flower arrangement look bigger, richer, and more complete, adding volume and texture.*

Another disruptive factor was public holidays. Since we supplied flowers to diverse countries with different traditions, their public holidays often overlapped in unpredictable ways. Most farmers—and I hold nothing personal against them; many are truly great and intelligent people—often presented a challenge when it came to business: trust was a perennial issue. When demand surged higher than supply, many (though not all) growers would attempt to sell whatever they processed at the highest possible price. For instance, they might sell flowers graded as "Not for Export" to a random client willing to pay more, or even prioritize a new, higher-paying client over their long-term partners. My role, often a contentious one, was to convince them of the opposite: that a long-term business strategy, one that involved working with us—a company that took over 50% of their year-round production at standing order prices—

was fundamentally better.

We used to say in the fresh-cut flower industry that working with a grower is like playing with a boomerang: it always comes back to you. Growers who broke a deal, "hiding" production to sell it at higher holiday prices, would inevitably find themselves in a bind during the summer. When market demands plummeted and production soared, we, the loyal buyers, would naturally prioritize and support those who had supported us during the peak holiday seasons. The boomerang of loyalty always returned.

I became quite an aggressive client—not physically of course—but it was common for me, despite my executive role as CEO, to be directly in the field, helping our teams. I might arrive at a grower's farm, knowing he had some extra stock, and almost by force, load flowers onto our cooling truck with my team. Imagine: a CEO, dressed like a farmer, speaking their language, striding into a cold room, and simply taking baskets of flowers and loading them onto our refrigerated truck. Of course, everything was meticulously counted and paid for, but the sheer directness was startling. I vividly remember one Israeli grower, anticipating my arrival before Valentine's or Women's Day shipments, placing one of his farm employees at the farm gate. Their sole task: to inform the grading house and the farm manager the moment *"Yuly is coming!"* This was not just business; it was a psychological operation.

In this business, if you want to lead, you truly have to be tough—with growers, with airfreight agents, and sometimes even with clients. I'll elaborate on how to significantly reduce financial risk and cut down on paying claims by up to 80% later. But for now, suffice it to say, this demands fortitude.

Here, I must clarify something essential. Today, after almost 30 years of life and field experience as a serial entrepreneur, an executive in international trade, a security expert, and a contact combat and bodyguards instructor, I've combined all these facets. As a Corporate Speaker and Seminars facilitator, I help people **"Look, Listen, and Respond better"** to reduce risk and achieve success. The demanding, "aggressive" approach I just described might seem to contradict my previous chapter's emphasis on empathy and connection. Being an aggressive buyer, or a person arguing over a $100,000 claim from a client, or negotiating an $80,000 loss caused by an airline, still requires you to remain human. A gentleman, nice, friendly, forgiving, and very thoughtful. I will delve into this crucial balance in the next chapter.

*Learned Lesson: Strategic Aggression and The Boomerang Effect*

*In a volatile market, selective aggression, combined with unwavering fairness, can secure your supply. Don't be afraid to demand what you need, but always back it with integrity and a long-term commitment. Remember the "boomerang effect" of trust and loyalty: those who support you in times of scarcity should be prioritized in times of abundance. Being physically present and willing to get your hands dirty, even as a leader, builds respect and ensures supply when others are floundering.*

**Reflection and Wrap-up:**

**There is a line between being firm and being ruthless. This chapter is about learning where that line is—and how walking it with both strength and grace makes you indispensable. If you've ever wondered whether leading from the front really matters, ask yourself: when pressure hits, who do people want by their side—the one who points, or the one who pulls with them?**

---

*Being "tough" in business doesn't mean sacrificing your humanity; it means applying firmness within a framework of profound respect and genuine connection.*

---

# Chapter 24:
# The Human Touch in a Ruthless Business

## Beyond Toughness: Connecting Through Shared Humanity

Writing a book is certainly not a one-day task; it has been several months since I embarked on this one. During this time, I've met fascinating people, taken on new projects that brought with them fresh knowledge and more expertise. I recently returned from training an amazing couple—both executives and YPO members—in Tennessee. I was hired to provide Situational Intelligence and Security Awareness Training. By the end of the training, we had a relaxed, insightful chat, discussing mutual friends and various business achievements. Just before I left, Larry, the husband, came down with a book in his hands—a book he had recently written titled *"Don't Be A Stranger"* by Lawrence Perkins.

Now, don't misunderstand me: I'm not trying to sell you this book, nor do I have any financial interest in it. But this particular book immediately transported me back to the flower business, and even further back, to when I first founded my initial business at the tender age of 14 in Israel. I won't recount the entire book, but what Larry suggests, and his core method, is profoundly simple: <u>making connections</u>. Genuine human connections that will, in turn, bring you both business and immense joy.

Now, let's circle back to me and the flowers. Look, I completely get it. After my last anecdote, you might be thinking I was some kind of brutal mafia boss, storming into growers' cold rooms, fully armed, and "stealing" flowers. Not really.

Remember, in the previous chapter, I told you that in the flower industry, like in any other, it's like a boomerang: you throw it, and it always comes back to you. Now, it's not a secret that I was married before; my first wedding took place in Israel. A typical Israeli wedding averages around 500 guests. How do I know? I worked in wedding venues as well, as a barman assistant (during my college studies, while also working in security and a few other jobs). I've been to many weddings and met a lot of interesting people. So, our wedding was quite small, with "only" 270 guests, while the requirement by the wedding venue was a minimum of 300 people.

No, I didn't have many friends from high school or my IDF (Israel Defense Forces) service, but I had, and still have, many friends in the flower, cargo, and transport industries. It's almost unbelievable, but nearly 90% of the flower growers, airfreight agency representatives, airline representatives, executives from packing material factories, and even the two major growers from Kenya with whom I closed the first and most important growing contracts— whose farms I helped introduce into new markets and who subsequently became immensely popular—came to my wedding in Israel. By the way, that wedding was also a main starting point for my career elevation and the crucial decision to open a subsidiary company for our Israeli firm in Kenya.

So, how does one cultivate a situation where almost 90% of your business- or work-related network attends your personal wedding? It's quite simple, rooted in the values I learned growing up.

I was born in the USSR, where values and respect for elders are instilled differently. And to be honest, I truly appreciate my mother's efforts to raise me that way—to remember and care for the people we love, to nurture friendships and family connections. Since I was a child, I made it a point to call people I knew and wish them a happy birthday on their actual birthday, not weeks or months later.

I used to call most of the women I knew and wish them a Happy Women's Day.

Well, back in the USSR, I was a little boy and didn't yet have a large network of women. In a century and a country without the luxury of digital devices, it was easy to remember or manage a small, paper-made phone notebook with connections and important dates. And I was young, with a great memory that hadn't yet been adversely affected by social media and mobile devices.

I applied this very same approach to my business network. I not only knew and acted upon a grower's birthday, but I also knew when his wife's birthday was, and even his kids' and grandkids' birthdays. Every once in a while, we would go out and eat together, talking about everything that was not related to business. If a grower needed help, I was genuinely there for him. Not just out of duty, or because I was "playing" a business-friendship game, but because it truly mattered to me, and I knew they would do the same if I ever needed it. This mutual respect and genuine care formed the bedrock of our relationships.

I'll bring one specific example to life.

One of the airline representatives who regularly helped us with our shipments from Israel, a man named Gil (name changed), invited me to his grandson's birthday party. I knew this invitation wasn't just because I was a significant client, providing him with good cargo capacity. At the same time, I went to that birthday not because Gil was trying his best to get me more space in needed aircraft during peak times. I bring this example because I vividly remember a specific case that tested our bond. Just a few days before I was invited to the party, Gil, at the very last moment, unexpectedly removed—or "cut"—30% of my crucial shipment from an aircraft. This was perishable cargo, with a very short "vase life" and extremely sensitive to any temperature changes. I was absolutely furious! It was an early morning flight, departing around 2:00 AM from Tel Aviv to Amsterdam. From there, we had booked trucks that were supposed to collect the shipment and distribute it all over Europe, in some cases with further connecting trucks. Imagine splitting a shipment: it's not just leaving some boxes of flowers behind; it also necessitates creating entirely new sets of documentation, customs forms, invoices, and packing lists. Not to mention the potential disaster for someone's wedding in Bulgaria, where a client of mine, who imported flowers there, was supposed to sell those flowers to a wedding florist for critical decorations.

When I received the email about the space problem and our boxes being offloaded from the airplane back to the airport cold rooms, I literally jumped out of my bed, still in my pajamas and home slippers, and rushed to the Ben Gurion (Tel-Aviv) Airport cargo area. On the way, I called

Gil and our managers, demanding everyone be there in 30 minutes. When Gil, clearly annoyed, commented: *"Yuly, it is 11:00 PM and I am in my bed,"* my response was immediate and unambiguous: *"Gil, if I can jump out of my bed and drive wearing pajamas to your office, you can too!"* And I promptly disconnected the call. The confrontation was direct and uncompromising, yet the underlying human connection ensured that despite the heated moment, our long-term relationship would survive and even thrive.

*Learned Lesson: Cultivating Genuine Relationships Beyond Transactions*

*In any business, true, long-term success is built on genuine human connections, not just transactional exchanges. Go beyond professional courtesies; invest in understanding and caring for your partners as people. Remember key personal dates, offer support beyond business needs, and be present in their lives. This personal investment builds a foundation of unshakeable trust and loyalty that can weather even the most intense conflicts and supply chain crises. Being "tough" in business doesn't mean sacrificing your humanity; it means applying firmness within a framework of profound respect and genuine connection.*

**Reflection and Wrap-up:**

**You don't have to choose between being human and being**

effective. The biggest results often come not from tighter contracts or better systems—but from deeper connection. When the stakes are high, it's not your title or tactics that people remember; it's how you made them feel. In business and in life, connection is the currency that never devalues.

# Chapter 25:

# The Chaos of the Cold Room

## Unpacking Offloads and Unforeseen Complications

What happened next, I'll divide into two fronts. The first, and the reason I chose to be physically present, was to get an accurate, firsthand account of what actually happened during the offload—what was removed from the plane, and what remained on board. You might suggest barcodes, but back then, that technology wasn't reliable enough to be trusted in high-stakes logistics.

To truly understand the scale of the problem, let's zoom out and imagine the heartbeat of our operation: our company's cold room. Once flowers were collected from growers, they were sorted, processed, and carefully packed into boxes tailored to each client's precise specifications. From these packing lists, we generated invoices and customs clearance forms. These documents were then sent to our clients' customs brokers across multiple countries. Many of those brokers had their own—let's call them "creative"—ways to clear goods or minimize taxes. In such a landscape, precision wasn't optional. Every stem counted.

What I haven't yet mentioned is that all this documentation had to be completed a fixed number of hours before the flowers even reached their final destination. We were racing the clock the entire time. And the clock was always winning.

Let's summarize: flowers packed, paperwork complete, boxes loaded onto our refrigerated trucks. We dispatched the necessary documents to our airfreight agents—Gil among them—along with cargo instructions. Then, customs brokers in Holland, Russia, and elsewhere received their files, along with transport companies scheduled for the last-mile delivery. The flowers were delivered to Ben Gurion Airport's cargo cold rooms and loaded onto their designated flights. At this point, the web was fully spun. Any disruption would unravel everything.

And then, without warning, some of our boxes would be offloaded. Arbitrarily. No explanation. No warning.

Why? A few all-too-familiar reasons.

One: another airfreight agent had better ties with the airline's cargo director and managed to squeeze in more of their own client's goods.

Two: the flight was a passenger flight with shared cargo space, and a family traveling with ten oversized suitcases pushed us out.

Three: if there was a pet on board, the animal's temperature requirements overrode everything else, and perishables like flowers were the first to be sacrificed.

So back to the chaos. Cold rooms in cargo terminals—particularly in this part of the world—were often logistical nightmares. And before you assume Europe is more sophisticated, think again. The only place I ever witnessed truly flawless efficiency was the Aalsmeer Flower Auction in Amsterdam. That place was a marvel. I remember standing frozen, mouth open, as I watched carts of flowers gliding through a massive space with Swiss-watch precision. If you're ever in Amsterdam, skip the Red Light District. Go see Aalsmeer. It's an operation worth studying.

But back to Ben Gurion. Our flower boxes were rarely consolidated onto a single *pallet*. Some would be on one pallet, others on a separate trolley, and so forth. When a decision was made to offload cargo, entire pallets or carts might be returned to the cold room—without notice, without tracking, without logic. No real-time alerts. No chance to make live adjustments.

And that's where the real pain began. If customs paperwork weren't so rigid, if time weren't so unforgiving, we could have afforded to absorb the delay. But we couldn't. Our clients expected precision. Our competitors offered alternatives. Delays meant lost trust. Lost trust meant lost clients. And lost clients meant invoices we couldn't collect.

*A pallet, in this context, refers to a flat wooden or metal platform used to group cargo, making it easier to load and unload goods from aircrafts, trucks, or warehouse shelves.*

Technically, the freight agent was supposed to manage this chaos. But I had learned early on that relying solely on their records was risky. Their logs could be incomplete or flat-out wrong. Whenever boxes were offloaded, every document—packing list, invoice, Phytosanitary certificate—had to be recreated instantly.

### Learned Lesson: The Cost of Chaos and Unforeseen Delays

*The final mile of logistics, especially with perishables, is the most vulnerable. Delays, documentation errors, and surprise offloads don't just disrupt operations—they undermine trust. These failures often stem from a mix of systemic flaws (limited cargo space, customs bottlenecks) and unpredictable human behaviors (favoritism, overbooked passengers). When you lose visibility, you lose control. And in the world of perishables, control is everything. To survive, build contingency systems. Don't just prepare for perfection. Prepare for the mess.*

Reflection and Wrap-up:

Every entrepreneur craves control, but real leadership reveals itself in disorder. Your role isn't to dodge chaos— it's to enter it, organize it, and lead through it. When others blame, you take charge. When others hesitate, you move. Logistics isn't just about systems; it's about decisiveness in foggy moments and clarity under pressure. The cold room was never just a place—it was a battlefield. And I learned that leading well in that space didn't come from titles or degrees. It came from being the one willing to show up when everything was on the line.

# Chapter 26:

# The Midnight War Room

## Strategic Thinking Under Pressure and The Human Element of Crisis Management

When I arrived at the airport cold room—still in my pajamas—I knew there was no time to waste. I immediately issued clear, direct instructions. Gil and a few others were tasked with tracking down the offloaded boxes, comparing physical inventory with the master shipment documents, and creating an updated picture of what had actually made it onto the flight. It was our war room, and this was our battle plan.

Before we could revise a single document, I had to make one of the most important decisions in the entire export chain: What would we do about the missing boxes? That answer required more than logistics—it required people skills, intuition, and deep knowledge of my clients.

I knew who would lose their temper over a delay. I knew who could wait a day without throwing their entire supply chain into disarray. I knew whose flowers were mission-critical, and whose could be reduced temporarily. And most of all, I knew who I could call at 2:00 AM and count on them to listen.

Take Anna from Vladivostok. A week earlier, I'd called her to congratulate her 12-year-old son, Misha, on winning his school's swim competition. That simple, heartfelt call turned out to be invaluable. When the emergency hit, I called her again—this time with bad news. I needed to cut her order by 50%. But because I had earned her trust, and because I knew how her logistics chain worked, I could reassure her that the remaining flowers would reach her the very next day. I had enough leverage with our consolidation partners in Amsterdam and enough goodwill with the truck company that handled her route. That truck company, by the way, was run by a man I'd shared several long lunches and whisky shots with during the International Flowers Expo. Relationships matter. Especially in chaos.

This book isn't about glorifying myself. It's a field guide, rooted in real experience, for how to survive and grow under pressure. The lesson? You don't just need strategy—you need speed, memory, and relationships. These are assets forged over time, often in places that have nothing to do with business plans: a war zone, a back office, or a roadside diner at 3:00 AM.

While corporate manuals emphasize Business Continuity Plans and Risk Assessments, reality demands something more immediate. Most plans end up on shelves. But crises play out in seconds. If you want to lead, you must think five steps ahead—and be someone people trust when the heat is on.

Back to Gil. After we'd fixed what we could and I'd made sure every change was documented, I unloaded my frustration. He took it, to his credit. Maybe it was the absurdity of two CEOs in pajamas yelling over boxes of roses in a freezing cargo terminal. Maybe it was just what needed to happen. Either way, once the dust settled, we found ourselves at one of those 24/7 shawarma joints next to the airport. Still in our pajamas. Still cold. But finally able to laugh.

That's the human part of leadership. And it shows up when you least expect it.

Another story comes to mind. Hary, one of our flower growers, called and asked if I could meet. We'd just had coffee at his place a week earlier, so this felt odd. I was slammed, prepping for a major Kenya trip. I asked if it was important. He hesitated, then said yes.

I drove to his house. Hary—normally stoic, solid— was in tears. His wife had been diagnosed with aggressive cancer. He wasn't calling me as a business partner. He was calling as a friend.

I couldn't postpone my trip, but after that, I carved out time for him every chance I got. Because that's the kind of person I want to be. And because that's the kind of relationship that can't be built in the boardroom.

Leadership isn't about shouting orders. It's about listening when it matters. It's about remembering birthdays, noticing silences, and showing up when others would reschedule. My mother raised me to see people as people—not titles or transactions. If someone needed me, they could call. No calendar link required.

I remember the early 2000s, working security at a hospital. Friends would call me on a Thursday night: "Yuly, last-minute plan. Camping by the Jordan River. Want in?" If I could switch shifts, I'd be there by midnight. We'd grill, laugh, sing. Thirty tents of joy and connection.

I miss those days.

Now, everything's formal. Want to see a friend? Send a calendar invite. Hope they're available next month. That's not connection—that's convenience masquerading as commitment.


*Learned Lesson: Proactive Crisis Management and Empathy as a Strategic Asset*

*In a crisis, speed matters. So does wisdom. But never underestimate empathy. True leaders don't just command—they* connect. *When you cultivate real relationships, you earn flexibility, grace, and resilience. And when you treat people as people—not roles—you build a network that carries you through the storm. Contracts are useful. Loyalty is priceless.*

**Reflection and Wrap-up:**

**The midnight war room wasn't just about saving shipments—it was about preserving trust. Leadership under fire isn't just about intellect. It's about instinct. And empathy. Real strategy starts with knowing your people— clients, partners, team—and leading with both strength and heart. Whether it's flowers, freight, or friendships, the lesson is the same: be decisive, be human, and never underestimate the power of a well-timed shawarma.**

# Chapter 27:

# The Air Cargo Conundrum

## Navigating the Geopolitical Maze of Logistics

This chapter takes us full circle, back to the pivotal decision that changed everything: my first direct growing contract in Kenya. But before we get there, let me unpack one more piece of the puzzle.

I've already laid out the headaches we faced with local Israeli growers and detailed several real-life logistical nightmares. But there was another recurring problem—one that might seem trivial, even absurd, until you're the one watching your cargo get offloaded to make space for someone's golden retriever.

Yes, I'm talking about passenger flights. A family of ten going on vacation with oversized luggage? That eats into our cargo space. A tourist who buys a seat for their dog? Say goodbye to your flowers. Each extra suitcase or animal cage meant a reshuffling of cargo priorities. And guess what got bumped first? Perishables like flowers.

Zoom out for a second. Open up a map. Now overlay it with the political complexity of the Middle East. From that lens, Israel is essentially landlocked in terms of logistics. Exporting goods—especially time-sensitive goods—comes down to two options: sea freight or air freight. Sea freight for fresh-cut flowers was, at that time, not viable. (Though I later dipped my toes into a sea-shipping project that was as ambitious as it was exhausting.) So, that left us with air cargo.

Now imagine this: most of our buyers were in Russia, Ukraine, Kazakhstan, Uzbekistan—places I broadly group under "Russia" for simplicity—and Europe. Some even operated from the U.S. or Australia. Often, these buyers sourced flowers from multiple companies and countries. Many consolidated everything in Amsterdam, where shipments then splintered into trucks or connecting flights for final delivery.

From Israel, direct cargo flights to major Russian cities like Moscow, Kiev, Tashkent, or deep into Siberia were rare. This forced us to rely heavily on passenger flights. But that meant fighting for space, not just against other exporters, but against vacationers, pets, and the unpredictable whims of airline logistics.

There's an old saying: *"Don't put all your eggs in one basket."* So I didn't. I booked capacity across three to four different airlines for a single shipment. Seven tons on Aeroflot airlines, Fifteen tons on El Al. Twenty on Uzbekistan Airlines, which routed through Tashkent before delivering to Moscow. It sounds excessive—until you realize it was the only way to ensure the flowers made it at all.

And still, despite this juggling act, I can't remember a single shipment that went smoothly. Not one. We were always scrambling—always begging, bargaining, or bullying our way into securing space. Every week, every shipment, it was the same brutal competition.

It was unsustainable.

This logistical chokehold—this constant stress and fragility—wasn't just a problem. It was the catalyst. It drove me to rethink the entire model and seek out a more stable, efficient solution. That solution, as you now know, started in Kenya.

### Learned Lesson: Overcoming Geopolitical Logistics and Diversifying Capacity

*The constraints of geography and geopolitics aren't just abstract concepts—they dictate your daily operations. When infrastructure limits your options, adaptability becomes your survival tactic. Use multiple partners. Embrace complexity. But don't fool yourself into thinking that competing for cargo space is a long-term strategy. Reliability is the real currency. And for me, that meant pioneering a new route—one special flower box at a time.*

Reflection and Wrap-up:

This chapter isn't just about freight. It's about freedom—the freedom to build a supply chain that works for you, not against you. In the chaos of disrupted cargo, it's easy to lose sight of strategy. But every delay, every offload, every frantic call to a freight agent was sharpening my resolve. Logistics isn't just about moving goods. It's about moving forward. And for me, that journey led to Kenya—not just as a grower, but as a lifeline for the entire operation.

# Chapter 28:

# "Catch": The Rose that Changed Everything

## How One Bi-Color Rose Sparked a Market Breakthrough

"Catch" wasn't just a name; it was a revolution in a roses A bi-color T-Hybrid rose with fiery red and golden-yellow hues, it changed shade and brilliance depending on the altitude and location of its production. While farms across many countries attempted to grow it, the Kenyan-grown Catch rose stood out for its exceptional quality—and our clients noticed.

After another fruitful trip to Kenya, I managed to do something bold: I convinced Mr. Combos of the Subati Group to sign an exclusivity agreement with us. It meant that four of his farms would only sell roses exclusively to us, as well as other flowers, for the Russian market. This was massive. We now had sole rights to a flowers that everyone wanted but could only get—from us. Every time a client tried to go around us and talk directly to Elizabeth or the Subati team, they were redirected back to our company. That exclusivity helped us dominate a critical, growing segment of the market.

## Planting the Seeds of Profit: My First Growing Contract

But, exclusivity means nothing if you don't have volume. Riding high on momentum—and with the full trust of the company owners behind me—I proposed something bigger: that Mr. Combos plant additional hectares of Catch roses just for us. We'd agree on the price in advance, we'd commit to buying everything that met export standards, and we'd help him expand his capacity. In short, it was a pre-buying agreement before the product even existed.

By 2008, around the time of my wedding, I was running the entire flower operation independently. And this deal? It was mine to lead. That growing contract was more than a purchase order—it was a crash course in commercial agriculture, legal frameworks, international contracting, and risk mitigation. I didn't call it "raising capital," but that's what I was doing in spirit. I didn't speak the language of venture funding, but I understood instinctively how to reduce risk by getting buy-in upfront.

So, I did what made the most sense: I booked a flight to visit key clients and showed them the flower, the farm, and the deal structure. I gave them the chance to commit early. Many did. That gave us the security we needed to push forward.

*Learned Lesson: Proactive Risk Mitigation Through Client Commitment*

*When you're committing resources before the product even exists, de-risk your investment by securing your customers first. Pre-selling or early agreements can help fund the production phase and shift your financial exposure into a shared opportunity. You don't need to speak the language of capital markets to act like an investor—just think like one.*

### Reflection and Wrap-up:

**The story of Catch is the story of leverage. Not financial leverage, but relational and strategic leverage. A superior product gave us attention. A bold contract gave us exclusivity. And early client commitment gave us security. The real growth didn't come from selling a flower—it came from owning the flow. Catch was more than a rose. It was our first real proof that we could shape the market instead of chasing it.**

# Chapter 29:
# The Art of the Deal: Georgian Open House Diplomacy

How Saunas, Wine, and Straight Talk Sealed a Game-Changing Agreement

Here's something I didn't share earlier, but it's crucial: the best business doesn't always happen in boardrooms or over polished PowerPoint presentations. Sometimes, the most transformative deals unfold in places where titles are left at the door—like a smoky Georgian open house or a steamy Russian banya.

Picture this: a traditional Georgian restaurant just steps from Red Square in Moscow. Heavy wooden tables, trays of grilled meats, deep bowls of khinkali dumplings, and pitchers of homemade wine. There I was, surrounded by future partners and flower buyers, presenting an idea that hadn't fully taken root yet—exclusive access to a flower that wasn't even grown.

That night, over laughter and toasts, my proposal came to life. I offered them the first cut—literally—of Catch roses that we'd plant exclusively for them. In exchange, they'd commit to multi-year agreements with fixed pricing and volume expectations. These were handshake-style agreements—formalized later, yes—but born from trust, face-to-face conversation, and a few shots of chacha.

This wasn't the usual business dinner. There were no laptops. No suits. No egos. Just people eating with their hands, wiping sweat from their brows, and talking straight. I told them the truth: I had never done this kind of deal before. I wasn't a grower. They weren't growers. And even the farm we were partnering with—Subati—had never grown flowers like this, for clients this demanding. It was all new. But, it was also real.

Each side had skin in the game. My clients got first access to an in-demand product with price certainty. Mr. Combos got a guaranteed buyer. I got the rarest asset in our industry: control over both production and demand. And I sold, with margin, a product that technically didn't exist yet.

### Learned Lesson: Authenticity Closes Deals

*Don't underestimate the power of showing up, being human, and telling the truth—even if that truth includes what you don't know. People don't just buy the product. They buy into you. Especially in emerging markets or industries built on relationships, authenticity often carries more weight than credentials.*

Reflection and Wrap-up:

The Georgian dinner table taught me something no classroom ever could: *trust is built in shared spaces, not spreadsheets.* I didn't need to be perfect—I needed to be honest. And that kind of honesty created a bridge between clients, growers, and my vision. The deal we made that night didn't just launch a product. It launched a new way of doing business—one where laughter, risk, and respect sat at the same table.

# Chapter 30:
# Out of Curiosity: Deep Dive into Flower Production

Why Knowing Your Product—Petal to Root— Matters More Than Ever

The first thing you must include in your risk assessment is this: know your product. Intimately. Completely. At a granular level. Every stem, every centimeter, every nuance.

I've said it before, and I'll say it again—I'm not a grower, and I'm definitely not an agronomist. But this first growing contract forced me to learn fast. And what I learned became foundational to every future success.

### Starting at the Source

The grower didn't just plant flowers randomly. First, they had to order the "Catch" variety from a breeder. Breeders are the origin point of new flower varieties— companies that experiment, refine, and release plants into the market. It's a world of its own, and later, I worked directly with them to forecast demand, shape planting strategies, and even co-develop future hits. But back then, I was just beginning to understand how the game was played.

A few essential terms I learned quickly:

- Budwood: The DNA of your product. Budwood is the stem section containing vegetative buds used to propagate new plants. It's how you get consistent, high-quality clones that stay true to the desired variety.

- Agrobacteria: The invisible saboteur. This bacteria causes crown gall disease in roses, creating ugly tumors that can destroy entire greenhouses. In this business, a "greenhouse" often means an acre or more. If agrobacteria spreads, your entire crop is at risk.

## Production, Length, and Yield—The Business Side of Beauty

In business, beauty isn't enough. You need numbers. You need strategy. That's where stem length and yield come in.

In the global flower trade, stem length is measured in centimeters (except in the U.S.). Most export-grade flowers range from 40cm to 80cm. Sometimes, for special events, we'd ship roses as long as 1 meter or even 120cm. But the sweet spot varies depending on your market.

In Europe, 40cm to 50cm stems were most popular. But in Russia and the former Soviet Union, buyers wanted length— 60cm to 80cm was the gold standard. That meant if we planted using the traditional "Catch" yield, we'd be stuck with too many short stems that no one wanted.

A Sample Traditional Yield for 'Catch' Might Look Like:

- 40 cm – 25%

- 50 cm – 40%

- 60 cm – 20%

- 70 cm – 10%

- 80 cm – 5%

That might work for Europe. But for Russia? It was a losing formula.

### Solving It With Altitude

Subati had a secret weapon: altitude. They had four farms at different elevations. At my request, they planted our "Catch" roses at the Subukia farm—2200 meters (7218 feet) above sea level.

That shift changed everything. The cooler climate and different plastic covering on the greenhouses extended the stems. Suddenly, we had:

- 40 cm – 10%

- 50 cm – 20%

- 60 cm – 40%

- 70 cm – 15%

- 80 cm – 15%

A perfect fit for our Russian clients.

We did lose a bit of the deep red color, but the improved length made it worth it. Even the 40cm stems—officially "waste" in our model—found a home, because I never left product on the table. I always found a buyer.

### The Yield Tradeoff
Of course, there was a catch with "Catch."

At lower-altitude farms like Lake Naivasha (1884m) or around Nairobi (1700m), a grower might get production of 220 stems per square meter per year. But in Subukia? Just 170 stems in some varieties it could go down to 120 stems. That's a significant reduction.

Yet again, the pricing made it all worthwhile. Our cost per stem at 60cm from Kenya was just $0.14. The same from Israel? $0.30. Ecuador and Holland? Even more. And remember—our Kenya roses were brighter, longer-lasting, and had far fewer claims.

### Margin or Miracle?
Some people might say a 300% markup is outrageous. But I

ask: is it theft—or is it simply smart business at the right time, in the right market?

The truth is, my success wasn't built on exploitation. It was built on insight. Kenya didn't yet understand the value of their product in our niche market. I did. So I built a bridge between a high-quality supply and a high-paying demand—and made that margin work.

These lessons didn't just help me in flowers. They helped me launch other ventures—like my 2023 homemade food brand, "A Taste of Home Kenya." Within weeks, we were in Nairobi's top hotels and supermarkets. The muscle memory of product-market fit, logistics, branding, and strategic partnerships? All learned from flowers.

*Learned Lesson: Deep Product Knowledge and Market Segmentation for Profit*

*Understand your product at a granular level, from physical traits to yield under varying conditions. Align production with market-specific preferences—because higher volume doesn't always mean higher profit. Value comes from insight, not excess. What seems like an outrageous margin to some is often just the reward for deep knowledge and smart segmentation.*

**Reflection and Wrap-up:**

**Know what you're selling. Not just the category—roses or**

software or food—but every detail that influences performance, cost, an appeal to your customer. When you understand those variables, you can customize your supply chain, maximize your value, and turn a commodity into a competitive advantage.

That's how I took a flower that no one believed in and turned it into a premium product with guaranteed buyers. The power wasn't in the petals. It was in the planning.

> *If there's one thing I've learned, it's this: if you've got the right mindset, no fear of failure, and the ability to learn fast—you can do wonders.*

# Chapter 31:
# Setbacks and Strategic Diversification

## Turning Delays into Launchpads for Innovation

It was late 2006 or early 2007. Our ambitious planting contract for "Catch" was not yet underway. First, I received news that a breeder had sent infected plants—tainted with agrobacteria. Thankfully, the Subati farm manager was sharp and promptly sent them back. Then, delays struck again: something went wrong with the specific greenhouse meant for our exclusive production.

I didn't wait. I flew to Kenya for a round of intense meetings. But surprisingly, these meetings didn't flag any major red lights. Nothing indicated our growing agreement was at risk.

Still, I couldn't just sit back. I was buzzing with energy—my brain a cyclone of ideas. By this point, I was fully managing flower exports from both Israel and Kenya. Orders were growing steadily. Garbage-quality roses from Israel were phasing out, and our Kenya exports were scaling up.

## Side Note: Unsung Heroes of the Flower World

I realize I haven't yet talked about other flowers and green fillers. Let me pay tribute to them now. While the roses from Israel were, as I called them, "garbage," Israel produced amazing Lisianthus (Eustoma), Sunflowers (Helianthus), Carnations, Aralia, Aspidistra (with and without stripes or dots), Asparagus (the kind you don't eat), and various types of Lilium—with one to seven bells, scented or unscented. I could go on for pages. It's funny—I still remember many of these varieties, even seven years out of the game.

## While Catch Was Delayed, I Diversified

Instead of waiting helplessly for "Catch" to launch, I threw myself into other projects. If there's one thing I've learned, it's this: if you've got the right mindset, no fear of failure, and the ability to learn fast—you can do wonders. This waiting period wasn't wasted. It became my proving ground for diversification and strategy.

The Magical Formula: Slashing Logistics Costs by Up to 30%

Here's a secret that changed everything: freight charges are based on two things—actual weight and volumetric weight.

- Actual Weight is obvious. You check your bag at the airport, it goes on a scale. If it's overweight, you pay.

- Volumetric Weight is where it gets interesting. It's calculated based on how much space your item takes up. If you ship a tiny lipstick in a shoebox, you're paying for the shoebox's size—not the lipstick's weight.

The formula: Length x Height x Width (in cm) ÷ 6000 = Volumetric Weight (kg)

Example: Let's say you pack a 5-gram lipstick in a shoebox (35cm x 25cm x 13cm).
That's: (35 x 25 x 13) ÷ 6000 = 1.89 kg

So even though the lipstick weighs next to nothing, the airline or freight forwarder will charge for nearly 2kg. At $15/kg, that's $28.35. If they charged based on actual weight, it would be about $0.45. That's a 6,200% difference!

And here's the kicker: most freight companies will charge whichever weight is higher. So if you're not paying attention to volumetric weight, you're losing money—fast.

## My Competitive Edge

Once I understood this, I redesigned our packaging to reduce wasted space. I optimized every box, every layer, every pallet. That move alone saved us up to 30% on logistics. Even more, it gave us a selling point for new clients: better prices, faster deliveries.

This wasn't just a logistics tweak—it was a strategic differentiator. It allowed us to turn "air" into profit.

### Learned Lesson: Mastering Volumetric Weight

*Always calculate and optimize for volumetric weight. It's the silent killer of profitability for light, bulky goods. Learn the formula—Length x Height x Width ÷ 6000—and redesign your logistics accordingly. Turning wasted space into savings is one of the simplest, smartest ways to increase margins.*

## Reflection and Wrap-up:

**Even when a major contract is delayed—or even fails—you can still move forward.**

**My Catch contract was in limbo, but that didn't stop me. I expanded into other flowers, improved our logisti**

and locked in new clients. Every delay was an invitation to learn, adapt, and build a more resilient business.

The key? Stay moving. Diversify smart. And always look for the inefficiencies others ignore. That's where your edge is hiding.

# Chapter 32:
# The Gerbera Revolution

## Smart Packaging, Smarter Sales

Israel was, at one point, a major Gerbera flower grower—not necessarily in sheer volume, but renowned for its exceptional quality. Later, I successfully ran a trial of growing Gerbera in Kenya, though our partners ultimately focused on roses, and Gerbera production expanded through other growers.

Traditionally, Gerbera were packed in what we called a "Penal box." A full Penal contained 300 Gerbera, arranged in five trays, each holding 60 Gerbera. The biggest issue with this Penal was its volumetric weight. While Gerbera are not very heavy flowers, the actual weight of a full Penal was around 13 kg, yet its volumetric weight was almost 20 kg. This meant that for every Penal 300(flowers) shipped, exporters and growers were overpaying for 7 kg of empty space—"air," as we called it. We sometimes found ways around it through good relationships with airline representatives, but it still represented a significant loss for everyone involved.

The second problem was the packaging itself: the Penal was made of plain white craft paper, completely opaque. There was no way to see the Gerbera inside without opening the box.

I decided to change both: the box size and the box type. After several months of cutting trays, reshaping Penals, reducing and adding holes with office scissors right in my office, I finally created a ready-to-ship solution—a working sample. The final, crucial test was ensuring it didn't compromise flower quality under any conceivable circumstances or risk factors. For the next two weeks, I was literally throwing boxes on the floor in our cold room, taking them out, and putting them back into the cold store. I was attempting to simulate a real shipment environment with extreme temperature changes and the brutal handling that often occurs in airports. After two weeks of this abuse, I opened the Penals and was completely satisfied with the results.

Next, I met with the manager of our main box manufacturer, Ahia. Our factory was located in Haifa, Israel, about 50 km from our offices, but Ahia was always ready to meet at any point. When I showed him my redesigned box, he was genuinely impressed, especially considering his factory was one of the largest box suppliers in Israel, with about 90% of our growers sourcing their boxes from him. While I didn't manage to reduce the overall Penal size, by cleverly relocating and redesigning the holes in the flower trays, I managed to create space for one more layer of

Gerbera. And by slightly lowering the side borders, one more tray could fit into the Penal. The result was revolutionary: the actual weight of such a new Penal was now virtually identical to its volumetric weight. This meant we would no longer pay for empty space. Those 7 kg of emptiness were now filled with profitable flowers. Make your own financial calculations: the final price of Gerbera could either go down for the client, or companies like ours and the growers could significantly increase their profit. The smart approach was a balance of both.

Now that I had optimized the packaging for efficiency, I wanted to tackle branding. Or more accurately, I wanted to increase sales by improving visibility and creating a situation where our Gerbera would stand out among all others. I applied the same principle later when designing the packaging and branding for my "Taste Of Home" company. When you walk into a massive supermarket the size of my flower company's warehouse, and stand in front of a huge, very long refrigerator filled with yogurts, what do you look at, or what do you pick up? The answer is clear: the one that's different, the one that's "shouting" from the shelf, *"Hey, I'm here! You can see me, you like me, now you want to touch me (the packaging)!"*

With Gerbera, my idea was to create a transparent box with a plastic cover (plastic at that time) so you could directly see the beautiful flowers inside. The inspiration for this came from Israeli Duty-Free shops, which were pioneering this type of transparent packaging.

Ahia, from the factory, agreed to make a prototype of such a box. My plan was to ship it to different clients in various locations with diverse weather conditions. It was crucial for me to gather opinions and feedback from a broad range of real-world scenarios. After about a month, I used the sample boxes and shipped them to clients. The feedback was overwhelmingly positive, and I was incredibly happy.

Unfortunately, that specific project never fully came to fruition in its original form, but I gained an incredible experience and immense satisfaction from the process.

After the successful trial, Ahia called me for lunch, where we discussed moving forward and printing those new boxes for us exclusively. To cut a long story short, Ahia explained:

*"Yuly, making a new type of box exclusively for you would cost a fortune. First, you'd have to apply and register a new product under your company—a very long, expensive, and complicated process. Then, even if approved, there's no guarantee that another grower wouldn't simply add one more extra hole, or one less, and legally be allowed to use almost the same boxes while you'd borne all those expenses. Lastly, to print such boxes, we, as a factory, would have to create a new template (cutting plates), whichis also very expensive."*

I don't remember what we ate, but the meeting was productive. After a short conversation with our company owner, I reluctantly dropped that specific idea. However, it pushed me toward a new adventure: repacking and optimizing boxes specifically for Kenya. The lessons learned were invaluable, laying the groundwork for future innovations.

*Learned Lesson: Packaging Innovation as a Profit Driver*

*Innovative packaging isn't just about aesthetics; it's a direct driver of profitability and market differentiation. By optimizing internal space, you can significantly reduce volumetric weight, directly cutting logistics costs. Furthermore, visual appeal and transparency can dramatically increase product visibility and desirability in a crowded market.*
*Even if a specific innovation doesn't fully launch, the process of problem-solving and prototyping yields invaluable experience and can spark new, impactful*
*solutions.*

**Reflection and Wrap-up:**

**This chapter wasn't about just boxes or flowers. It was about the mindset of optimization—of seeing hidden inefficiencies and choosing to tackle them creatively. While others accepted the penalty of volumetric weight or the dull anonymity of plain packaging, I saw a chance to**

innovate. I didn't wait for perfection or permission—I got my hands dirty with scissors and samples. The final product might not have hit full scale, but the value of testing, trialing, and pushing beyond "how it's always been done" paid off many times over in my next ventures. That's the power of curiosity combined with strategy.

# Chapter 33:
# Roses: The Impact of Pack Rate and Handling

You already know that the number or amount of products you put into a package directly impacts price, client attraction, market leadership, and ultimately, your revenue. Kenya, at the time, struggled with every single one of these factors.

Allow me to unpack that topic in a very descriptive way. As you sit at your home, office, or public place reading this, imagine a single stem of a flower that perhaps sits in your vase right now. Before you purchased it from a shop, it was most likely packed in a bunch of 10–20 flowers. That bunch was then placed inside an SFK—a craft paper sleeve that protects the flower heads from technical and weather damage. This type of packaging had a significant impact that I will reveal in just a moment. As you can imagine, that bunch of, say, 10 roses inside an SFK could be delivered to the shop in two most common ways: one "on water," the second one "dry" in a box.

The "on water" method is common if a farm or grower isn't very far from the wholesale distributor or the shop, and it usually doesn't involve air or sea transportation, but mostly road delivery. Sometimes farms put flowers in water baskets or trays with a special water solution (designed to increase vase life) and ship flowers this way. These flowers arrive fresher; the flower head might even grow a bit and open, so the flower is immediately ready for sale. No boxes are involved.

The "dry" method, however, requires boxes. The bunches of roses, along with many others, were packed into a box and might be repacked multiple times during their journey from the grower to the flower shop. We call this handling.

At the beginning of this book, I mentioned a crucial principle: *"As more people touch me, faster I will die."* Every time people touch flowers—starting from the farm (before and after harvesting, transferring from a greenhouse to a grading house and a cold room, packing before flight, unpacking and repacking in a flower auction or by resellers, and so on, until it comes to you)—the more people touch them, the shorter their life span will be in your vase. So, now you understand the critical role of boxes and packaging.

Fortunately, Kenya, at that time, struggled with every single step in this process. I am incredibly proud to say that I personally changed the entire market, revolutionized packing methods, and successfully rebranded the entire Kenyan fresh-cut flowers market.

If someone were to call me a liar (and I've met a few who have), well, I have only one simple answer: "Write your own book and tell your side of the story."

Dear reader, I'm not comfortable with excessive self-praise, but I also believe it's important to acknowledge meaningful achievements. I feel this warrants sharing.

As mentioned, Kenya struggled with many problems. Let's start dissecting them one by one. I am sure from this, you can learn a lot to improve your own business.


Back in 2006, and I'd argue almost up to 2012 when I relocated to Kenya, the local paper production was far from international standards and presented a very poor image. The Single Faced Kraft (SFK) paper, used to wrap flower bunches, was an ugly brown color, incredibly soft, and lacked any moisture resistance. As it absorbed humidity from the flowers during shipment, it would quickly degrade, looking precisely like a used napkin after you've blown your nose. Sorry for the blunt analogy, but that's precisely how it looked upon arrival after a 14-day journey.

This brings me to a crucial business principle: *if you want to truly improve, get up from your chair, visit your final client, see what they see, feel what they feel, and then improve based on their actual needs.* Growers in Kenya only saw a "nice," brand new SFK in their packing houses and even in their cold rooms. I, however, witnessed mashed, damaged, and hideously presented flowers in my clients' wholesale cold rooms across Europe, Russia, and other markets. If you live in the USA or Europe, you might now see in large grocery stores like Whole Foods Market or ShopRite, and in major flower shops, beautifully designed boxes and SFK from Ecuador, Colombia, and local production—packaging that makes you want to discover more. This stark contrast was unacceptable and had to change, a process that took significant time and effort.

Like the SFK, the box industry in Kenya struggled immensely. Available boxes came in only a few (two or three) generic sizes, with uniform poor color printing quality and, crucially, abysmal paper quality. This included the glue used by factories to bind layers and the insufficient number of paper layers in each box, both for the top and bottom. If I recall correctly—it was a long time ago—the bottom of such a box typically had three layers, and the cover only two. These boxes frequently broke apart in many cases even before arriving from the farm to the main international airport in Nairobi, Kenya, Jomo Kenyatta Airport, ready for export.

When airlines stacked pallets with 50 or even a hundred of these fragile boxes one on top of another, clients used to receive "Kasha." "Kasha" is the Russian word for porridge, a dish I personally love to eat. In this context, however, it was a very different kind of "porridge"—one that could even ruin my appetite after opening such a box of flowers following a long shipment, enduring many changes in temperature and humidity conditions across the globe. The flowers were literally mashed into an unrecognizable pulp.

For years, I tried to change this in various ways. I worked closely with most packaging material factories in Kenya, who were very supportive with numerous trials, but all of them consistently refused to invest in better paper quality and change their suppliers. Ultimately, it happened, but it took time and a radical solution.

In the interim, the solution came from Israel. Yes, that's not a typo or a grammatical mistake. The Yama factory, located near Haifa city in Israel, was a producer of high-quality boxes. During another meeting with Ahia, we struck a deal: I would provide the graphic design (something I had never done before) for our Kenya-specific boxes, and they would print and prepare a full container of boxes, which I would then ship by sea from Haifa, Israel, to Mombasa's port in Kenya.

Now, as you plan your next strategic move for your own operation, allow me to offer some advice: *before jumping into a running river, first immerse yourself and learn to manage the current.* Before embarking on such an adventure of printing boxes and shipping a full container to Kenya, I conducted at least 10 different trials.

This was a period when I was traveling between Africa, Europe, and Russia almost every month. During my last few visits to Kenya, I purchased extra luggage space from the airline, and along with my personal luggage, I brought flower boxes from Israel—the very ones we used for exports from there. In Kenya, I personally went to trusted and loyal farms, packed the flowers myself using these new boxes, shipped them to our clients, and then was quick enough to fly from Kenya to our clients so I could personally receive the boxes with flowers and make all necessary assessments for both the boxes and the flower quality. This included rigorous vase life tests. The results were amazing! Not only did the flowers arrive in excellent condition, but our boxes also looked incredibly representative, with a significant lack of damage that would undeniably increase sales. I conducted these trials with different clients because they were located in various places and received flowers under different circumstances, using different methods and experiencing different weather. I vividly recall flying from Kenya to Holland to check boxes there (a halfway point), then from Holland to Siberia in Russia, verifying if our flowers still resembled flowers and not icicles, and finally to Moscow.

Only after these extensive trials, and after conducting all the necessary financial analyses and negotiations with airlines and trucking companies that delivered the flowers, did I arrange for that crucial box shipment from Israel to Kenya.

Unfortunately, I don't remember the exact amount of boxes we shipped back in 2007, but despite all the logistical risks involved—including the looming threat of Somalian Pirates and the laid-back "Hakuna Matata" perception prevalent in Kenya—after almost two months, our first container of new boxes finally arrived at Mr. Combos' office in Nairobi. From that point, the journey toward saving 30% of transportation costs had truly begun. The next chapter brings us even closer to the full solution.

### Learned Lesson: Innovation Requires Rigorous Testing

*Never implement a major change without comprehensive, real-world testing. Personally oversee trials, replicate challenging conditions, and gather feedback from every stage of the supply chain, especially from the final customer. This hands-on approach, though demanding, provides irrefutable data and the confidence needed to scale bold innovations.*

Reflection and Wrap-up:

What looks like just paper or packaging is often your brand's first impression. If that first impression is soggy and torn, your customer won't care how beautiful the flowers inside are. In business, the smallest overlooked details—like the quality of paper—can destroy a premium product. It took a stubborn will, global testing, and a healthy dose of chutzpah to solve what others had accepted for years. When no one local would meet the need, I went international. Sometimes leadership means skipping incremental fixes and making bold, full-scale moves. That's how you turn a used napkin into a brand statement.

If economic shifts, make it impossible to sell your product. Don't just cut costs—create something new. Something that carries the same spark, the same charm, but is priced for the reality your customers are living in now.

Innovation isn't just about features.

It's about timing, empathy, and the courage to evolve when the world does.

# Chapter 34:

# New Agreements with Transport Providers

## Optimizing the "Pack Rate"

Just in case you forgot, airlines were charging exporters based on volumetric weight or actual weight, whichever was higher. This specific issue primarily covered shipments from Kenya to Europe and other destinations.

However, flowers undertook a very long journey even before that—from the farm to the airports, and then from middle locations (like Europe) in transit toward their final destination. Usually, transit trucking companies charged per kilogram. Let's use an example: $2.5 per kg from Holland to Russia (Moscow). Doing the math—which, to be honest, I struggled with greatly in school and genuinely disliked, yet became quite adept at when it came to business, down to the micro-level—I concluded that if the trucking companies would charge us per pallet (where we could fit 30 of our Israel-sized boxes), it would be most beneficial for us. Several intense meetings yielded results: I secured agreements that from then on, they would charge us, or our clients, per pallet. Later, with the 2008 economic crisis, I negotiated that down even further, to charging per box. They began calculating and billing us on a per-box basis.

Additionally, each shipment involves different types of documentation, such as an Air Waybill (AWB), Phytosanitary certificate, Customs forms, and various others. Each of these documents costs money, usually per shipment, but sometimes per box.

Finally, the last lesson about cost-saving, an experience that proved incredibly helpful years later when I was advising other companies on export and, more recently, started my food production business in Kenya in 2022.

Let me take you back to the roses pack rate for a moment. I'll add details I didn't mention before. Below is the average pack rate of how growers and exporters used to pack flowers before the change I implemented, and many still do, even as I write this book.

Old Roses Pack Rate:

- 40cm: 400 stems / box (volume weight 15kg, actual weight 9kg)

- 50cm: 280 stems / box (volume weight 15kg, actual weight 9kg)

- 60cm: 200 stems / box (volume weight 15kg, actual weight 9kg)

- 70cm: 140 stems / box (volume weight 15kg, actual weight 9kg)

By introducing the new, stronger boxes that preserved and protected flowers better, and with a specific grading and bunch packing method I implemented (which I cannot disclose in this book because I still do consulting), you can calculate the saving yourself. Here is the new packing rate:

New Roses Pack Rate (My Innovation):

- 40cm: 1000 stems / box (volume weight 24kg, actual weight 28kg)

- 50cm: 500 stems / box (volume weight 24kg, actual weight 28kg)

- 60cm: 400 stems / box (volume weight 24kg, actual weight 28kg)

- 70cm: 260 stems / box (volume weight 24kg, actual weight 28kg)

- 80cm: 180 stems / box (volume weight 24kg, actual weight 28kg)

Three significant savings happened at once:

1. Saving on all documents: Fewer boxes meant fewer documents per shipment.

2. No more paying for empty space: We were no longer paying airlines and truck companies for "air" because the actual weight exceeded the volumetric weight.

3. Price drop per box: By negotiating to pay truck companies per box instead of per kilogram, the price dropped by double.

On average, I cut the transportation cost down by $0.03 per stem. In case you think that's too minor, let me surprise you and repeat what I mentioned earlier: on average, an exporter of fresh-cut flowers would make a commission of $0.03 per stem. Later, by 2016, this dropped down to just $0.01 or $0.02. My innovation effectively doubled (and often quadrupled) the profit margin per stem for my company and growers.

The entire idea with the boxes was like an absolutely separate project, and ideally, a separate department would have been needed to manage it. It wasn't just about producing boxes in Israel, distributing them in Kenya to every single farm, managing stock remotely (since it wasn't easy relying solely on farm workers), and planning production accordingly while monitoring strikes, pirates, and other risk factors. It also involved consistently visiting every farm, training their teams on how to pack and use the boxes properly. The "Hakuna Matata" mentality simply didn't work here. Working with countries like Kenya, where wages are low, the education of people working in agriculture is minimal (if at all), and the perception might be "stealing an apple and risking a job to sell it today outside a farm gate for an extra 10 cents is better than keeping a job."

You're probably saying now, "Yuly is biased." Maybe I am, or maybe you just don't have 17 years of experience working and building a business in such an environment. I could be blamed for many things, but not for this: the export flower project I founded increased Kenya's flower presence from a negligible 0.05% to almost 50% in some markets, directly and indirectly creating thousands of jobs, expanding villages, building roads, hospitals, and much more.

But, back to boxes. It was an almost a continuous cycle: I was in Kenya on average every 2 or 1.5 month, sometimes staying in Kenya for a week to a month. I could train people at the farm to work with boxes, after 2-3 weeks they would forget, if I was still in Kenya I would go there again, if I was already back in Israel, I would have to wait for my next trip in average, every 1.5 months.

This went on for several years until I officially launched the Kenya company in late 2008, with its own office and our dedicated local people who could oversee operations consistently.

## The Box Project and the Tunnel of Surprises

The box project not only put me in a leading position in the market — it also unexpectedly opened the door to new opportunities through a dark tunnel of uncertainty and surprise.

I'll jump forward for a moment. I had just returned from a trip to Kenya, where we were still negotiating how and when *Catch* would finally be planted. Then came a quiet message from the market — a whisper about instability at Subati Group and possible ownership changes.

Subati's management, including Elizabeth, kept assuring me that everything was stable: planting was on track, orders were secure, and our recently signed exclusive sales agreement for the entire former USSR block would continue as planned.

But my gut told me otherwise. Something was off.

Just a week after returning home, I booked another flight back to Kenya. I couldn't explain it logically — it was pure instinct. And, as in many parts of my career, instinct proved right again.

A month later, I received an email from Ravi, introducing himself as the *new owner of Subati Farm*. He explained that during the ownership transfer, the previous team hadn't handed over any client lists, orders, or contracts — all previous agreements were void.

He said that while walking through the farm, he noticed boxes in the packing house printed with my company's name and contact details. That's how he found me.

It was one of those moments when the market shifts overnight, and you have only two choices: panic — or adapt faster than anyone else

*Learned Lesson: Continuous Oversight and Cultural Adaptation for Implementation*

*Innovation isn't enough; flawless implementation is key, especially across diverse cultural and operational environments. Be prepared for the ongoing challenges of training, compliance, and adapting to local work cultures (e.g., "Hakuna Matata") to ensure new systems are consistently followed.*
*Establishing a dedicated local presence is often crucial for sustained success and realizing the full benefits of large-scale operational*
*changes.*

**Reflection and Wrap-up:**

**Saving money in logistics isn't about cutting corners—it's about mastering every centimeter of space and second of**

process. The right box size, the correct packing method, the shift from per-kilo to per-box rates—none of these things are glamorous, but they're what keep businesses alive. The secret to scaling is in the details. When you obsess over efficiency and back it up with local adaptation and oversight, you don't just improve profits—you redefine what's possible in your industry.

---

*Innovation isn't just about features. It's about timing, empathy, and the courage to evolve when the world does.*

---

# Chapter 35:

# Navigating the Great Recession and Redefining the Rose Market

## The Great Recession of 2008: Impact on the Flower Market

The 2008 financial crisis, triggered by the bursting of the US housing market, had a cascading effect: stock prices plummeted, unemployment soared, and the global economy slowed significantly. Russia, a major market for us, was not immune, and the fresh-cut flower market felt the profound impact. I believe this was the first time Russian consumers were forced to reconsider and reshape their traditional preference for large-headed flowers. I began to observe a subtle but undeniable transition towards slightly more affordable products. At the same time, the deeply ingrained mentality of a Russian man gifting a charming 10 cm (3.93-inch) rose head bouquet to his beloved woman remained powerful.

My gut feeling and intuition told me two things would happen:

1. Reduced Bouquet Size: Previously, a man might buy a bouquet of 20–30 large-headed roses, along with cosmetics, chocolate, and perfume. Now, financial realities would compel him to reduce the number of stems in the bouquet, perhaps down to 9 or even 7. Those with stable finances might still add the perfume and cosmetics, but the flower component would shrink.

2. Demand for New Solutions: Simultaneously, a significant portion of the population would no longer be able to afford such luxuries. They would need slightly smaller roses, cheaper alternatives, or entirely new solutions that could still capture the essence of a beautiful gift.

This situation brought a crucial business lesson into sharp focus:

If economic shifts make it impossible to sell your product... don't just cut costs—create something new. Something that carries the same spark, the same charm, but is priced for the reality your customers are living in now. Innovation isn't just about features. It's about timing, empathy, and the courage to evolve when the world does.

This was a profoundly impactful experience and a helpful lesson for developing a resilient business strategy.

*Learned Lesson: Innovate, Don't Just Cut Costs in a Downturn*

*Economic downturns demand innovation, not just cost-cutting. Instead of simply making existing products cheaper (which can devalue your brand), focus on creating new products or services that align with the changed economic realities and evolving customer needs. This requires empathy for your customer's new circumstances and the courage to pivot your offerings.*

**Reflection and Wrap-up:**

**Sometimes disruption reveals more than it destroys. In this cas the recession exposed not just fragility, but opportunity. It taught me that maintaining relevance in any market means constantly tuning in to what people are facing—and then having the guts to meet them there, even if it means letting go of your previous assumptions. The size of the rose didn't change the love it expressed—just the cost of delivering it.**

# Chapter 36:
# The New Subati Owners: A Call for a New Adventure

The change in Subati's ownership brought what could be perceived as bad news. Indeed, if you don't know how to navigate challenges and learn from mistakes, such changes can feel entirely negative. In my case, however, it was a clear call for a new adventure.

Here I was again in Kenya, this time having coffee in an amazing UK-style farmhouse in Subukia, just a few kilometres from the Equator sign, with Ravi and Naren Patel—the new owners of Subati Flowers.

Ravi and Naren, with surprising candor, allowed me to share all the details of the previous agreements we had with the Subati Group. By the end of our discussion, they informed me that as the new owners, they were canceling all previously achieved exclusivity agreements and were no longer interested in planting the "Catch" variety. I was also informed that the prices we had agreed upon with the former Subati Group were no longer available, and this was non-negotiable.

However, by this point, I had already gained considerable knowledge in communication, empathy, sympathy, and body language skills. These were skills I had successfully honed not only in security settings but also, crucially, in business negotiations. Temporarily, we agreed to maintain the current flower supply flow at the existing prices for the next few months. This grace period would give me time not only to prepare my clients for the impending changes but also to secure more growers in Kenya, thereby mitigating risks and balancing our average revenue and pricing.

Ravi, surprisingly, liked the idea of planting roses together under a new agreement. For both of us, it offered stability: for him, a clear path to grow his farm faster with guaranteed supply; for me, a sustainable flow of flowers under agreed prices and conditions. This was the true test of the experience I had gained.

### Learned Lesson: Leverage Soft Skills in Negotiations

*Beyond hard facts and figures, soft skills like communication, empathy, and body language are invaluable in high-stakes negotiations. These skills can help you maintain relationships, secure temporary agreements, and buy crucial time to adapt to unexpected challenges, even when faced with non-negotiable demands.*

Reflection and Wrap-up:

Transitions often seem like endings, but they're frequently beginnings in disguise. I could have walked away frustrated, seeing only what was lost.

Instead, I engaged with new ownership with openness and resolve, leveraging my experience and soft skills to turn uncertainty into opportunity. This moment reminded me: every new chapter in business starts with a conversation—and the courage to keep showing up at the table.

# Chapter 37:
# "Red Lipstick with a Yellow Rose?":
## Understanding Market Nuances

My two years of intensive work had given me a deep understanding of the flower market. I knew exactly what type of roses clients liked: the preferred head size, the desired color, and even the way a flower opened, as different roses open in different ways, and have varying petal shapes that can in many cases, deter clients.

*I can offer you a few examples you can use to consider when planning your next product, whether it's a physical good or a service:*

You've noticed I frequently refer to Russia; this is simply because they were my major client. Based on old Russian tradition, the number of flowers in a bouquet should always be odd. An even number of flowers is typically reserved for funerals or for bringing to a grave. At the same time, a pure yellow rose traditionally emphasized a break-up and symbolized sadness. There was a strong belief that if you gave a yellow rose to your woman, your relationship would likely not last long and would soon lead to a separation. There's even a very popular song: *"Yellow Tulips, a Sign of Break-up."*

When preparing the "Catch" contract, I already knew it would be a 4–5 year commitment. Now, I was tasked with finding flowers that the new Subati ownership would plant, varieties that would remain in high demand for at least the next five years. I've always believed in a personal touch with clients and partners. Therefore, I spent the next few weeks traveling extensively through Russia, Ukraine, and Holland, trying to discern not only new trends in flowers but also in perfume, fashion, and cosmetics. Women, at least the majority of them, are very particular about what to wear and what colors will look nice together. As for us men, it was often less complicated. We used to love red roses and would give them to our women, and it was hard for us to understand why our beloved might be happier receiving a bi-color pale pink rose while she was wearing dark pink lipstick and yellow shoes to a theater show, versus just a classic red rose.

*A note:*

*Please don't argue but — it is a simple fact: women's brains are different.*
*Not better or worse, just different — in how they think, communicate, and even how their brains have evolved over generations, dating back to very early, survival-driven times.*

*There's an excellent book I often reference in my corporate workshops on communication and navigating rapid change — **How***

*Women Can Succeed in the Workplace by Valerie A.*
*It offers great insight into how these differences can become*
*strengths when understood and applied well.*

The results of my extensive research suggested that clients still desired big-headed roses, but they also needed a cheaper price point, given the financial crisis. Crucially, the market was ready for a new product.

### Learned Lesson: Know the Culture to Know the Customer

*Market knowledge isn't just about data—it's about understanding the culture, the habits, and even the emotional symbols that shape customer behavior. If you're introducing a new product or planning a long-term investment, spend time in your target market's shoes. What looks like a rose to you might symbolize a break-up to them.*

## Reflection and Wrap-up:

**Listening, observing, and immersing yourself in your customer's world is the secret advantage few take time to master. In the end, the customer doesn't buy wh at you sell—they buy what they feel. And feelings are deeply cultural, emotional, and contextual. You can't Google that. You have to go live it.**

> *Don't save on a lawyer—but don't forget: Your lawyer knows the law. You know your business. The smartest decisions happen where those two meet.*

# Chapter 38:
# The Rise of Spray Roses

My research pointed to an emerging trend: Spray Roses. A Spray Rose stem is characterized by many small rose buds growing on a single stem, typically 7–12 individual buds or small flowers. In 2008, Spray Roses were not popular in Russia, and if I'm not mistaken, only one farm in Kenya was growing them—and in very small quantities. The majority of their production was destined for the Holland Flowers Auction.

I compiled a list of about 15 rose varieties, including both single-head and spray roses, that I believed would be interesting for the market over the next five years. Unfortunately, the process offered by Ravi, both for the planting contract and for regular sales, was very high. I would say Ravi clearly saw the immense potential in the Subati farm and, consequently, increased prices by three times, effectively opening the door for fierce competitionand canceling the exclusive sales agreement I had signed with the previous Subati Group company owner

Looking at the numbers, I made a decisive choice: we would only pursue a contract for planting Spray Roses. The single-head roses contract, which was also offered and approved, was taken up by our first competitor, who saw it as a new opportunity.

Spending significant time at the breeders' greenhouses around Lake Naivasha, Kenya, I carefully selected my initial list of spray rose varieties from Interplant Roses. *(Later, I also worked with other breeders).*

## Understanding Flower Breeders

Earlier in this narrative, I promised to explain more about breeders. A breeder is a company or individual who develops new plant varieties through cross-breeding. This process takes time, involves testing for strength and consistency, and results in the creation of unique plants for market sale. Growers then pay a royalty fee per stem or plant sold, under a licensing agreement.

My first list of chosen spray rose varieties included:

- Yellow Babe: yellow

- Babe: orange (color varies by altitude and greenhouse plastic)

- Abeba: light yellow

- Rubicon: red

- Pink Flash: pink with white stripes

- Snowflake: white

This was the starting point of a project that would grow significantly over the years. By 2012, I encountered two new promising spray varieties that hadn't yet been named. Being a proud father of twin daughters, Alisa and Victoria, I wanted to name both. However, Girish, one of our key partners, had his own naming preferences. We ultimately named one rose Alicia (after my daughter Alisa) and the other Shivani (named after someone in Girish's family).

We negotiated favorable terms and exclusivity for these spray roses, made more attractive by the still-profitable margins and our transportation cost savings. The growing contract was structured as a three-way agreement between our clients (who agreed to purchase at set terms), us as the buyers from the farm, and Subati as the grower.

Drafting the growing agreement was one of the hardest, yet most educational, tasks of my career. Israeli growers shared advice, but we still missed a few crucial points. Eventually, we hired a lawyer to review the contract, but legal advice alone wasn't enough. The real insight came from blending legal rigor with on-the-ground business experience.

A critical miscalculation arose: the color distribution of the first delivery. The breeder sent only yellow, orange, and white plants, instead of the full rainbow mix we had planned. Worse yet, the red and pink plants were delayed and, when they did arrive, two batches were diseased with Agrobacteria and had to be destroyed.

This disrupted our entire production plan. Our clients expected consistent color mixes for events and holidays. A bouquet of only yellow spray roses had little appeal in the Russian market, where yellow roses were as I mentioned earlier, associated with break-ups. The delay in having a full color range set us back nearly 18 months.

During that challenging time, I found temporary buyers in Europe, where yellow roses carried no such stigma. It was a stressful but eye-opening chapter. Meanwhile, I continued growing the overall business and managing exports from Israel, Kenya, and Ecuador, refining my systems and building the next opportunity.

### Learned Lesson: Build In Contingencies and Know Your Supply Chain

*No matter how airtight a contract looks, your operations will only be as successful as your weakest logistical link. Never assume the breeder, farm, or even nature will follow your timeline. Include contingency clauses, staggered planting, and oversight checkpoints to prevent misalignment in your supply chain.*

Reflection and Wrap-up:

This chapter taught me something simple but powerful: A good idea is only as strong as its execution. Vision must be matched with precision. And while passion gets you to the table, only relentless preparation keeps you in the game. Even a beautiful bouquet can fall apart if the colors arrive out of order.

# Chapter 39:

# Expanding Horizons – Opening a Consolidation Hub in Kenya

## The Need for a New Approach

Our operation had grown significantly, and competition in Kenya was escalating rapidly. Many companies began to work directly with growers, which led me to propose our next strategic move: *opening a consolidation hub*—a dedicated company in Kenya. My vision was to create a service that would function much like Amazon does today, combining products and consolidating shipments and flowers on a micro-level. This was a service that no one else in Kenya was providing yet.

Don't get me wrong, farms did combine flowers, but only from their own production. They certainly didn't mix varieties from different farms in the same box. As a client, you couldn't even put 'Freedom' roses and 'Sweetness' varieties in the same box, even if they grew on the same farm. Furthermore, you couldn't combine different lengths of flowers in the same box. *This rigid system was inefficient and costly for many buyers.*

The 2008 recession created a unique situation where many smaller flower traders began operating independently.

They were actively looking for ways to bypass the major import companies—my existing clients. Simultaneously, due to inflation and fluctuating currency exchange rates, our larger clients faced increasing pressure regarding payment possibilities and trust. If a client's credit line was once $100,000, it became very difficult to maintain that level of trust. At the same time, I strongly believe in partnership and a gentleman's word. I'm proud that I never poached a single client from my own clients, nor did I ever take an active client from the company I worked for after I resigned and moved to Kenya to open my own company in 2012. This stands true despite many rumors in the market.

It was three days after a major surgery when, from my hospital bed, drugged with painkillers, the owner of the company I worked for brought me my first laptop. Fueled by OxyContin and OxyCodone, administered every couple of hours by the doctor, I had a breakthrough. The pain medication actually helped me conceive the idea for "**Ultra Flo Ltd Kenya**" and structure its entire operation. All the while, I was still managing and monitoring our ongoing export staff remotely.

In September 2008, I traveled to Kenya (as a newlywed, no less) to officially register and establish this new operation. A word about Kenya at that time: internet speed was just fast enough to send a batch of emails that, after pressing the 'Send' button, would actually be delivered hours later, especially if they included documents or images. It was a test of patience!

### *Learned Lesson: Opportunity in Adversity*

*Major market shifts, like economic recessions, often create unmet needs and new opportunities. By understanding these shifts and having the courage to innovate, you can introduce new services or products that cater to a changed market landscape, even if it means building from scratch. Furthermore, sometimes your most creative ideas emerge when you're forced to think differently—even if it's from a hospital bed!*

## The New Operation: A Consolidation Hub Takes Shape

I was 30 years old, brimming with energy. The core idea was to create a central consolidation hub where we would receive flowers from various farms across Kenya. Our facility would meticulously control quality, and crucially, provide a unique solution for smaller companies. These clients needed pre-mixed, ready-to-sell flower varieties in single boxes, which significantly reduced their operating expenses (OPEX). They no longer needed large (or even any) cold rooms, storage facilities, or packing space. Instead, they could rent or purchase mini-vans and distribute flowers directly from the arrival truck at the destination country's airport to the flower shops.

These clients could now include up to five varieties of roses from different farms in one single box. We would meticulously check the quality, repack it according to our cost-saving logistic system, label it precisely, prepare all necessary documents, and then ship it directly to them — sometimes even including door-to-door delivery, though I wasn't always a fan of that last option.

Of course, these clients paid a higher price per stem and faced stricter payment restrictions than our major clients, which helped us maintain financial balance. But, reality and market demand dictated these terms.

Ravi from Subati, introduced me to Jessie, who was the Executive Director of Air Connection company in Kenya. Their warehouse and cold-room were strategically located right at the entrance to Jomo Kenyatta International Airport. We quickly agreed to work together. I secured an office in their building and a significant space within their cold room for our own operations. This was a strategically brilliant option for me. Every truck arriving with export production at the airport first passed by the Air Connection building, giving us priority access to flowers based on a Last In, First Out (LIFO) principle for quick processing. We had more than enough time to prepare shipments before each flight.

Within two months of my arrival in Kenya, we had a full operation up and running, with staff that included a dedicated packing team, QC personnel, a manager, drivers, and myself overseeing everything. I can't recall all the farms now, but I was working with most of the major and middle-tier growers: Subati Flowers, PJ Dave, Batian Flowers, Zena Roses, Aquila Farm, Uhuru Farm, Siera Farm, Sunbud, Veg Pro, and even some trials with Fontana Group, Carzan Flowers, Desire Flora, Waridi, and many others. I would confidently say that nearly 90% of Kenyan growers supplied to us.

Kenya was growing and developing very fast as a country, but the mindset and critical thinking skills of people working on the farms were still problematic. At some point, I grew tired of constantly running around to farms, teaching them how to pack properly in our new boxes. I found it more effective to move some of this repacking and quality control to our airport facility, keeping only the most manageable farms doing the initial packing for us.

Unfortunately, Kenya still couldn't produce good quality boxes, so we continued to import them from Israel. However, most of these imported boxes were now kept at our airport facility for our own usage, ensuring consistent quality control.

Two months later, it was time to move back to Israel. After ensuring that our local staff could manage the daily operations and that I could effectively monitor and manage remotely (Zoom didn't exist; we relied on Skype and emails),

I returned. But I came back to Kenya every few months, or whenever necessary.

I won't recount every single story or routine event, simply because they wouldn't offer much in terms of new lessons for you. It was mostly about maintaining operations, finding new projects, and striking new planting agreements—including a project to grow Gypsophila in Israel, which was my last project with the company I was working for at the time.

### *Learned Lesson: Centralization Creates Competitive Advantage*

*Consolidation is a powerful solution in fragmented, inefficient markets. By creating a centralized hub that added value through quality control, variety flexibility, and logistic efficiency, we provided essential services that helped smaller buyers thrive— while ensuring our own sustainability in a turbulent market.*

### Reflection and Wrap-up:

**The Kenya consolidation hub wasn't just a business expansion—it was a leap of strategy. It taught me the value of bold innovation, speed to execution, and staying true to your values. Even while operating under pressure, recovering from surgery, and working across cultures, we created something no one else had. And it worked. The lessons in logistics, partnership, trust, and creativity laid the foundation for everything that followed.**

# Chapter 40:

# The Thermostat's Tale – Unmasking Claims and Cold Chain Chaos

## The Challenge of Claims and Understanding the Full Chain

In previous chapters, I mentioned claims and how they work. What I want to highlight now is the absolute importance of knowing not only your product inside and out, but also the entire supply chain—from production right through to your client, and even understanding your client's behavior and their specific types.

No one likes losing money. If a client received 100 damaged stems and couldn't sell them, they naturally demanded compensation that reflected their potential revenue, sometimes even double it. This is what I call *"knowing your client."* This scenario played out with small clients claiming for 100 stems and large clients for 250,000 stems. I once took a last-minute flight to Ukraine to address a client trying to submit a claim for almost $80,000.

In many cases, claims in the flower industry were directly caused by adverse weather and improper storage conditions. Knowing these variables made it much easier for me to discern whether a client was telling the truth about damage or simply imagining it.

Consider this scenario: You have a product coming off the same production line, supplied under identical conditions to 20 different clients. Suddenly, one of them files a claim for a bad product. In many instances, you'd suspect the problem isn't with your production line or even your international supply chain, but with that client's local operations, or perhaps the market itself. In some cases, when markets were down, certain "blacklisted" clients would habitually send claims.

Very often, these claims were legitimate, but I knew the problem wasn't at the farm; it was with our airlines or trucking companies. Therefore, I sought out a company—I can't recall the name now, but back then there were only a few in the market—that provided thermostat loggers for air freight solutions. This device, placed inside a flower box, records temperature data on a paper film or, in later, newer versions, digitally. A client receiving damaged flowers could send me these records, allowing us to pinpoint exactly where the problem occurred: Was it between our cold room and the airport? From the airport to the middle destination (Europe, Russia, Australia, etc.)? Or from the transit airport toward the client's cold room?

Using these devices made it significantly easier to navigate claims and even fix underlying problems, as we now knew precisely where and what to repair or improve. They had only two disadvantages: the price per unit was high, making it financially unfeasible to include one in every flower box, and, critically, there was a delay in data reporting. This delay took me some time to figure out, and it's precisely the point I think would be valuable to share with you.

The thermostat device is located inside the box, and it records the temperature around and near itself. We encountered many claims related to inconsistencies in maintaining the cold chain by airlines, especially when flights involved hot weather countries and summer seasons.

Imagine this scenario: 100 boxes of your flowers arrive at the Tel Aviv airport cargo facility from your company's cold room, maintained at the necessary 4 degrees Celsius. Just before the boxes leave your cold room, you or your employee attach and activate such a device. In the airport, those 100 boxes are slowly—and sometimes with delays—offloaded from your truck, where the outside heat is almost 95 degrees Fahrenheit.

The boxes are offloaded, and while waiting for inspection by plant authorities and our freight agent, they are exposed to the intense heat. You might ask, *"Why not do this inside a cold room?"* It's a very good question, but the reality of airport logistics is different.

After some time, these boxes are finally moved by a forklift into a cold room. However, the heat has already affected the flowers in boxes loaded on the perimeter of the pallet. Slowly, that external heat begins to penetrate inside the box, where your thermostat device is located.

Next, the flowers are taken toward an aircraft, and in some cases, they will remain under direct heat again for a few more hours. Besides the condensation that will increase the chances for botrytis (a common fungal disease), the flowers also begin to "wake up"—starting to breathe and release their own metabolic heat.

Finally, after takeoff, the temperature in the aircraft cargo hold will drop. But this drop only affects your flowers and the device after they've already experienced significant temperature fluctuations.

This sequence of events created situations that no one could explain for quite some time, including airline representatives. After receiving a claim from a client and reviewing the temperature records, it would often show 12 degrees Celsius (8 degrees higher than the standard) two hours after the flight's departure. These records and the resulting misconception led to immense confusion about who would bear the loss: the grower, us, the airline, a transit company in Holland, or a truck company delivering flowers from Holland? I remember countless meetings and heated debates with airline lawyers and representatives.

This went on until one day, a grower suggested we conduct a trial together, creating a "game"—an imaginative process to simulate the journey. We used a few boxes with flowers as samples, taking them by tractor from his cold room to an open space simulating the aircraft loading process, and then back to his cold room, meticulously checking the temperature on the device at every step.

Only after that controlled trial did it become definitively clear: the perceived "temperature spike" inside the aircraft was primarily caused by the delay in the device measuring the temperature around itself versus the actual, fluctuating environmental conditions around the boxes or the entire pallet. The device only registered the internal box temperature once the external heat had gradually penetrated. This simple, yet crucial, distinction resolved all future debates and arguments once and for all.

*Learned Lesson:* **Data Reveals Truth**

*Invest in tools that provide objective data throughout your supply chain. While costly, precise data from devices like thermostat loggers can quickly identify problem areas, resolve disputes, and inform targeted improvements, saving significant money and relationships in the long run.*

Reflection and Wrap-up:

Understanding your supply chain isn't just good practice—it's a shield against risk and an amplifier of trust. By digging deeper into root causes and implementing technology to back our claims with facts, we could protect our reputation and relationships. The thermostat wasn't just a device; it was a symbol of accountability, precision, and the lengths we would go to uphold integrity in every stem we shipped.

# Chapter 41:
# The Moscow Subway and the Unseen Flow of Money

## A Disclaimer on Unspoken Truths

*Let me start with a clear disclaimer: This is not advice. It's not a call to action. And to be transparent—I was never personally involved in these types of operations.*

When you spend years navigating the business world, especially across borders and industries, you begin to see things differently. You hear conversations that don't make it into official reports. You learn to read what's not written. You start noticing patterns that, while never formally acknowledged, speak volumes.

In my work with flower growers—spanning continents, contracts, trade shows, and those long, revealing lunches—you eventually pick up on a recurring, unspoken truth:

*In some cases, the flower business can be a highly convenient vehicle for money laundering.*

Now, I'm not an economist or an accountant. But I've managed budgets, run operations, and even flagged errors in year-end audits. I've seen how numbers can move, and where the gray areas tend to widen.

Imagine this: *You run a successful business—a construction firm, a trading company, maybe a private finance operation. Revenue is strong. Tax exposure is growing. You look for a secondary venture—something real, visible, and familiar. You buy land. Build greenhouses. Start growing flowers.*

*Forecasted annual revenue? $5 million.*

*But one season, disease wipes out 25% of your crop. Or there's a sudden weather shift. The harvest drops. On paper, you've taken a loss—and with it, a legitimate reduction in taxable income.*

*No regulatory body is coming to count your stems. There's no forensic breakdown of how many stems made it to market. The flower business, in this way, offers plausibility—and in some circles, that's the most valuable currency of all.*

This isn't an exposé. It's a reflection. What interests me isn't the loophole—it's the psychology behind the structure. The ingenuity. The justifications. It's what happens when business, survival, and ethics all share the same greenhouse.

## The Cash Economy and My Moscow Commues

You might ask, how does this relate to a subway? Well, there's a direct link. The growers aren't the only ones who like their money; clients love it too. Because in the flower industry, the margin per stem is so tiny (it was better back then; nowadays, as of this writing, things are getting tighter), in most cases, a client—whether a major import company or a small entrepreneur—might have only a few US cents per stem margin. In the case of a big client moving from 300,000 to a few million stems per month, the situation might be better compared to a small entrepreneur selling up to 50,000 stems per month. Either way, both were motivated to save money and work with cash.

Just for a moment, I'll jump ahead to February 2014, the Ukraine revolution, also known as Maidan. This event triggered an economic embargo on Russia, blocking SWIFT transactions, freezing bank accounts, and so on. At that point, payment issues became even worse. But we're still around 2007 and forward, where clients preferred to pay by cash for their own reasons, including saving money on each transaction.

At some point, almost every trip of mine to Russia became a kind of money collection task. No, don't get me wrong, I wasn't part of some mafia or criminal organization collecting payments. But at the same time, let me ask you a question: Would you deny a cash payment from your client—"just printed" money offered to you when you're sitting in his office, or having a social lunch, or even clubbing with a bunch of them? Or would you prefer to wait three to six months for a bank transaction?

My intuition suggests we're on the same page. If a client places $20,000 out of the $70,000 he owes you on the table, you take it! Well, not everything is so easy.

Problem number one, and here my security and contact combat instructor skills became very necessary: the money was often given in Russian or Ukrainian currency. So, you have $20,000 in front of you, but in rubles. And again, there are two immediate problems.

First, you need to change it into USDs, Euros, or GBPs. Second, you have to somehow carry it with you and keep it in a hotel until the last step: figuring out how the hell you will transfer it or bring it with you on a plane. And one more problem, but not the last: that $20,000 was from only one client. You might visit 10 to 20 clients during that business trip, and you still have to do your actual business—finding new clients, striking new contracts, learning market trends, and so on.

Capitals and other major cities in Russia are as packed with traffic as anywhere else in the world. Therefore, I preferred using the subway. The Moscow Metro is incredibly comfortable and easy to use, unlike, for example, systems in the USA. In Moscow, trains arrive every two minutes, with almost no delays. You can actually plan your entire day of meetings and be everywhere on time. I'd start my day at 7:30 AM, take a train to the closest station, then a taxi to a client's warehouse, repeating the process for other locations, sometimes with the last meeting at 10 PM. *(Well, officially. Clubbing and socializing often continued until 5 AM the next day!)* The compensation for all this? New contracts, increased orders, and of course, good friends.

Back to the money, I promised to highlight more issues. I've lost count, but let's call this problem number four: when you get the rubles, you have to exchange them into another currency. At some point, the exchange bureaus started limiting the amount you could get, on average up to $3,000 per transaction. Now, after visiting five clients, I'd find myself with a significant amount of money in my computer backpack, moving underground on the subway.

Once in a while, I'd get up and go outside to the street to find a few exchange points to offload rubles, reducing the volume of "papers" in my bag.

The amount of stress I felt and the level of security awareness—combining all other possible types of awareness: intelligence, survival, situational, intuition, and gut feeling—was far greater than what I experienced while working in security, protecting people from possible terrorist attacks. This is when you truly get the best training in a real-world field.

## The Final Step: Moving the Money

The last step, or process, in that chain of actions was: what to do with all this money? As you probably know, you cannot cross a border or clear customs with more than $10,000 without declaring it. In my case, I didn't have a legal problem declaring it when returning to Israel, simply because we had all the necessary records, invoices, and statements for all that money. The problem was that I couldn't put our clients at risk. I definitely didn't want to fly with such an amount, and certainly not travel with it to Kenya, where the "Hakuna Matata" mentality for an expat— a white guy with nearly half a million USD in his bags passing by very hungry customs officers—is the worst and a nightmare situation, even for me. Funny enough, in 2022, I was stopped and almost arrested at the Kenyan Airport because handcuffs were found in my luggage. Apparently, handcuffs are not allowed in Kenya, and all my explanations that they were for training government personnel were unsuccessful. They were confiscated, and I was released after a long delay and wasted time. Weeks later, I got them back with a certain apology, but time was wasted.

## Money on the Move: Trade Shows as Unofficial Hubs

Moscow hosted a few major International Exhibitions. One was the Moscow Flowers Expo, where suppliers, airlines, and clients from all over the world gathered. Others were primarily where airline representatives and logistics companies exhibited and socialized. Soon enough, these events, besides their original purpose, became a kind of "Money Trafficking" hub.

Imagine this:

*You are  exhibiting or visiting the show, as are your client X, your flower growers from Ecuador, Colombia, Kenya, Holland, etc., along with KLM, Turkish Airlines, and many others, and also the factory that produces your packing materials. Your client visits you at your booth—a well-thought-out design with a back door and a double wall, used not only for keeping alcohol but also the...*

*My apologies, I forgot to mention the drinking habits in Russia, or rather, the volume of alcohol consumed during the two days of the expo—and not only by Russians! Usually, for three days of such an expo, we would keep 3–5 bottles of Whisky and Cognac for our visitors and clients.*

*A client comes to visit you, you talk, make jokes, have fun. Then another client comes; now there are three or six of you, and everyone knows each other. Ten minutes later, one of them suggests his throat is getting dry and needs some liquid. And now you find yourself drinking Hennessy with them. After 30 minutes, they go to visit and 'refuel' at the next narby booth where they also buy flowers. The exact same ritual will happen there. You? You'll find yourself with a new visitor and a few more shots. By t he evening, after the expo hall closes for visitors, many of the exhibitors from different countries, who have known each other for years in this business, will continue socializing before heading to a nightclub.*

*Again, I lost the main subject: the money. During that "tea" process, the client would give you his payment in cash, money that you would temporarily put in the double wall. Having been paid by your client, you could now pay your airline, truck company, etc., in the same way, right there, without a ny SWIFT transactions, bank policies, or paperwork. Money kept moving all those days, clearing balances and mitigating your own risk of being robbed or arrested, along with a few other not-so-friendly scenarios.*

During my almost 15 years in that business, I was lucky enough to still be alive, no more disabled than I am after my IDF service, and with only one case where almost $16,000 USD went missing. Eight thousand were stolen from me during a flight to Kenya, and the rest were confiscated, and I was almost arrested by Ukrainian Customs police, simply because I was very tired and forgot to fill out a cash declaration on my entry. I use this personal example in my seminars and corporate speaking engagements when talking about travel safety and security, and how to behave in airports and during flights.

# Key Takeaways from Part I

I hope you've learned from Part I that every journey begins before the title, the funding, or the recognition. It begins with curiosity, courage, and the willingness to act before you feel ready.

From my earliest lessons in discipline and situational awareness to my first experiences in global trade, the message was clear: you can't wait for permission to grow.

The stories in this section were not about perfect plans, they were about adaptability, observation, and the ability to learn faster than the problem unfolds. I learned that relationships built on genuine trust often open more doors than strategy alone, and that true leadership has little to do with rank. It's about staying calm under pressure, noticing what others miss, and moving forward even when the path isn't clear.

**Reflection and Wrap-up:**

**What started as a simple need for payments quickly became a complex logistical and psychological chess game. Navigating laws, currencies, cultures, and common sense was not just a business skill—it became a survival skill. And while the money moved fast, the real value was in the wisdom earned, the risks endured, and the global**

awareness sharpened with every step underground, every handshake, and every unspoken understanding. This chapter reminds us: business doesn't just happen in bo ardrooms. It often unfolds in shadows, subways, and side conversations—and knowing how to move safely through all of it can be the difference between success and disaster.

Resilience isn't built in a classroom; it's built in motion— through small daily decisions that test who you are when things get uncertain.

If there's one truth I carried from Part I, it's this: competence earns respect, but connection creates impact. The skills that make you effective in business are the same ones that make you human—empathy, observation, and courage.

The foundation for everything that followed—every negotiation, every risk, every global expansion—was laid here, in these first chapters of action and awareness.

# Part II:

# The Path to New

# Beginnings

Chapter 42:

# Resigning and Relocation – Reclaiming Life from Burnout

## The Weight of Global Operations

For a long time, I'd been seeking opportunities to relocate from Israel, dreaming of life in Europe or Canada. Even Kenya was under consideration. Yet, despite this desire for change, I'd simultaneously hit a wall. I came to a point where I felt utterly burned out in the company I was working for. I had reached the top, and the air was thin and stale.

*The smell of charcoal and grilled meat hung in the air. My twins, barely 8 months old, were laughing, sticky fingers clutching tiny plastic shovels. It was Saturday. A family BBQ. But my mind? Miles away. Negotiating a shipment delay in Holland. My phone, a phantom weight in my pocket, vibrated with another email. My brain, already spinning with AWB numbers and stem counts, tightened its grip.*

Burnout wasn't just a feeling; it was a physical weight. My eyelids were permanently heavy, my thoughts a tangled mess of logistics and deadlines. My body hummed with a low, constant anxiety, fueled by adrenaline and cheap coffee. I was a machine, efficient yes, but the gears were grinding, sparking, threatening to seize. Working globally and being available (or rather, reachable) 24/7 with a young person's resilience had burned me out five years later. I'm almost sure that if you are an executive or entrepreneur, especially if you're still young, say below 45, the feeling and experience of "jumping" from your seat or running toward your phone every time you hear a beep or receive an email or a message is not strange to you.

It wasn't until later, after moving to the USA in 2024, that an incredible client gifted me a book: *Gilded* **by Keren Eldad**. As I read, a chilling realization washed over me. What Keren described as 'overachievers' wasn't just a personality type; it was a state I'd been living in for years. A state that had quietly, relentlessly, stolen my life. Moving forward, millions of new ideas, a fear of not doing enough or lost opportunities, or emptiness once achieving a result, became my everyday life. Sound familiar? Great. Listen to my advice and the advice of many who almost lost everything, or almost everything. I am not talking about money; mostly everything, at least now that I am 47, is losing myself and losing the people I love and who love me.

Family birthdays blurred into a single anxious hum in my memory. BBQs with friends felt like obligations to endure between frantic email checks. Attending my two-year-old twins' activity should have been pure joy, but I was a ghost there. My eyes saw the colorful toys, but my mind was back in a cargo hold in Amsterdam. My fingers twitched for the familiar smooth surface of my phone, the constant stream of information a perverse comfort that shielded me from the harder work of being truly present.

*Imagine: 2 AM. Deep sleep. The sudden, shrill ring of your phone is like a physical blow. You're awake instantly, heart pounding. Your body is heavy, anchored to the bed, but your b*

*rain? Wide awake, terrifyingly clear. In seconds, you've accessed mental files: Client name. Order number. AWB. Airline. Departure. Landing. Number of stems. Prices. Every single nuance. It's a party trick of a brain that refuses to switch off, even when everything else is screaming for rest. True, keeping all this information could get more clients because your customer care and personal touch were above average, but it kills you from the inside, and to fix it can take years of therapy and result in broken families, kids who were taught to ride a bike by your personal driver or a maid.*

In 2010, I walked into our company owner's office, my hands slightly shaking, but my resolve firm. I told him: *"From now on, my phone goes into 'silent mode' after 8 PM until 7 AM. Saturdays. Off-limits."* The conversation was brutal. He argued about losing clients, demanding my 'expected' 24/7 availability. He pushed, demanded, but I held firm. Because I knew, with a chilling certainty, that if I didn't reclaim my life, even partially, I wouldn't have a life left to manage.

Finally, I gave him an example of how, just eight years before the technological advances of emails and Skype, people used to send faxes. And if a fax would arrive at your client's office after working hours, it would only be seen the next day. Yet, international trade existed and kept developing.

---

### The Digital Detox: A Hard-Won Battle

Suggestion: If you are planning such a move, you cannot just drop everything. Certain preparations and procedure adjustments should be made. A clear SOP (Standard Operating Procedure) should be created, and clients notified. It took me maybe a month to prepare everything, to restructure some processes, and notify clients.

And the day came. ~~May,~~ Friday, 8 PM, 2010. My phone and my brain switched off!

*What happened next could be a Hollywood movie script. First, a few clients were angry because they could not reach me. But after a week, they got used to it, and we did not lose a single client.*

*The second part was harder. If you go through a similar process, you should be mentally ready for it. You know those movies where a main character is addicted to drugs or alcohol? Where the first days you get very anxious, irritated, extra* emotional. Then, you cannot find peace with yourself, your skin is irritated

and itchy. After a week, you can't stop eating. Even if you used to hate steamed fresh broccoli, you will eat it nonstop.

Every loud sound around you, every child screaming from a neighbor's building, makes you almost cry.

From the second week, you force yourself to keep your phone away, at a distance in the next room from you. Yet, the desire to come close to it and touch the screen is so strong that it can replace your natural and human desire for sex.

Finally, after three weeks of these waking nightmares—the dying flowers, the missed emails, the imagined plane crash—something shifted. I opened my eyes after a full night's sleep, and the first thing I saw wasn't a mental checklist, but a tree. The same tree that had been outside my window for years, unnoticed. Its branches, heavy with leaves, formed a perfect, natural umbrella over my balcony. I sat on my sofa, the morning sun warm on my skin, and just listened. To the birds. To the quiet hum of a world that had kept turning, beautifully, without my 24/7 vigilance. In that moment, I didn't just see the tree; I saw a life waiting to be rediscovered.

This is where you realize that there is life around you, and you're ready to discover it again and get it back.

## Learned Lesson: Digital Detox and Rediscovery

*The initial phase of detaching from constant digital connectivity can be profoundly challenging, mirroring withdrawal symptoms. However, successfully navigating this period allows for a rediscovery of personal well-being, improved focus, and a renewed appreciation for life outside of work demands.*

*When people asking me about what I am doing or was doing, I can not say I was "Exporting Flowers", because exporting flowers sounds boring and generic. I am still looking for an answer- how in a sentence I could answer that question.*

# Chapter 43:
# Expanding Horizons and Facing New Risks

With the freedom from phone addiction, I started transferring more duties and responsibilities from myself to my team. I still created new projects and moved ideas not only in Kenya but also in Israel. This was also a time when I again considered exports from Ethiopia. Visiting farms, flower expos in Addis Ababa, and even conducting some trials, brought me to a final conclusion that the risk factors were too high and too numerous, and we did not have enough mitigation strategies and tools.

If you work with emerging markets, this section might be of interest to you. Using my experience, you can make your own decisions.

There were several factors for my decision:

- Political-Economical: Ethiopia is not an easy country to move money in and out of. Growers struggled to receive payments from their clients. The government was very strict, and every money transaction demanded extra paperwork. The same applied to making payments from Ethiopia outwards. Doing business with a high-sensitivity product like flowers, where many deals were last-minute and prepayments were a priority in the fast-changing economic reality, made this factor a major consideration.

- Mentality: In early chapters, I explained about the Kenyan people's mentality, especially in remote areas. In Ethiopia, on the farms, it was worse. Not impossible, but the outcome did not justify the effort.

- Logistics: Not much had changed since 2006 when I first checked the logistics. If you want to know if there are problems with logistics, try contacting local airlines, airfreight brokers, and other authorities you will have to involve during a crisis. Observe how they answer, respond, and how clearly they provide answers to your questions. More than that, you must be sure that they understand your questions and give accurate answers that reflect the topic. Finally, the air connection between Addis Ababa and the rest of the world was not optimal, and cold rooms at the airport were not well-equipped. The only way to deliver flowers from there to our clients was a flight to Liege, from there by truck to Amsterdam, which created extra risks and problems.

The last consideration was security, but I will skip it in this book.

Between 2010 and 2012, I was actively looking for a significant change in my life. Meanwhile, Kenya was well-explored, competition increased, and some growers, without mentioning names, decided to go behind our backs, contacting clients directly. I remember a year when I helped organize a trip for around 15 growers to Moscow to meet our clients during one of the Flower Expos. The Hennessy was consumed; I introduced growers to our clients; partying in a Moscow nightclub where you pay $10,000 to book a table was great. But the day after, four clients called me, saying a few growers had visited their warehouses and offered to work directly with them.

Anyway, my next project was to organize a direct cargo flight from Nairobi to Moscow. We almost formed a coalition of exporters to organize such a plane, but unfortunately, without significant success. The main reason was the price. We could easily load a full plane with flowers to Moscow, but the problem was there was nothing to bring back to Kenya. The plane would have to fly empty. That doubled the cost, and with my saving method of packing, the transportation cost of a flight from Nairobi to Amsterdam, and from Amsterdam a truck all the way to Moscow, was much cheaper than a direct flight.

As you could notice, just like you, I couldn't just keep doing the same thing; I always needed new fuel, which turned into several new adventures. Relocating to Kenya and starting the MAO Flowers company, slowly returning to security training and advisory—especially after the 2014 Ukraine crisis and some tax complications in Kenya—and just before moving to a new adventure of relocating to the USA in 2023, I launched one more and final business in Kenya: producing and distributing healthy homemade food, "A Taste Of Home." I won't explore that part in detail in this book, but I can say that using all my accumulated experience, it was much easier. In just two months after launching, we were supplying our products to most 5-star hotels and restaurants in Nairobi, selling our 13 products in supermarkets, and had received 9 out of 10 marks from executive chefs working in the industry.

### Learned Lesson: Knowing When to Walk Away

*Expanding into new markets requires more than just optimism and drive—it requires due diligence, operational awareness, and knowing when to say no. When risk outweighs reward and mitigation tools are lacking, the wisest decision can be not to move forward. True leadership is often proven not in pursuit, but in pause.*

## Reflection and Wrap up

This chapter reinforces the lesson that success in international business isn't just about chasing growth—it's about identifying the limits of opportunity and choosing your battles wisely. Logistics, mentality, legal systems, and partnership trust all matter as much as the product itself. While Ethiopia presented promise, it also posed significant challenges. Instead of forcing expansion, I pivoted. That pivot allowed me to refocus, launch new ventures, and reclaim energy for the next phase of my journey. Sometimes, not pushing forward is the greatest strategy for long-term growth.

# Chapter 44:

# A Turning Point – The Moscow Flower Expo and a Life-Altering Offer

## Moscow Flower Expo 2011: Security Gaps and Strategic Shifts

September 2011. Attending the Moscow Flower Expo in Crocus City Hall Centre, the same place where terrorists tragically killed over 130 people and injured hundreds on March 22, 2024, was a significant time for me. Just days before the exhibition—an event perceived as highly popular, with many countries sending representatives, including ambassadors—I was, as usual, preparing our booth. This involved ensuring florists and designers finished arranging flowers and posters, confirming that the models I'd hired understood their roles and had learned basic material about our company's activities, and even meeting friends, colleagues, and competitors.

At one point, I remember we couldn't find three boxes of flowers—samples we'd sent from Kenya and Israel to be displayed. I went to the backstage area, forgetting my exhibitor badge in our booth. Walking around, including the back lot, I was surprised by how easy it was for a stranger to get in without any security noticing. It immediately popped into my mind that if someone intended to attract international attention, that place and time for a terrorist attack would be a strategically optimal and easy target to penetrate, even bringing in ammunition and explosive devices.

Many years later, already living in Kenya and back in the security field, I conducted numerous security penetration tests. In 2023, I was even hired to monitor, and to provide an extra security layer for a top-level Africa Tech Summit where a former UK Prime Minister was scheduled to deliver a virtual speech, which was supposed to be secret and was considered a major threat.Eventually, he did not speak and the event was cancelled. It's always fascinating how event organizers underestimate security and how trusting they are of tech solutions versus human vigilance. I still strongly believe that technology alone cannot prevent, or that we cannot solely rely on technology to prevent, such attacks. At least in 2011, nothing major happened at the Expo, at least from a security perspective.

During the show, I met a farm manager from the Fontana Group who came to visit the expo. I had tried to work with this group of farms before, but we always had price and presentation disagreements, and it never worked out. I strongly believe that things happen in our lives at the right time and in the right place. Meeting that person, I noticed their readiness for a dialogue. I strongly believe the reason was the ongoing waves of the 2008 recession, which had affected global trade. The Fontana Group historically supplied mostly to the Aalsmeer Auction in Holland. They produced some of the best flower quality and had an amazing color range and shades; their year-round average price at auction was above most other growers in Kenya. One of their directors, who is also an agronomist—an amazing and very knowledgeable grower—was Girish Appana. Girish couldn't come to Moscow that year, but I was invited to visit their farms.

Entrepreneurs like you and I, we can't wait. We should be ahead of the curve. The next month, I was visiting the Salgaa farm, located in Salgaa near Nakuru town, close to Lake Nakuru in Kenya. Salgaa farm primarily grew small-headed roses, which were great for the new demand for cheaper and medium-sized heads. But Girish, with all his interest and desire to work with Russia, wasn't yet ready to reduce and adjust prices. The Fontana Group back then had farms totaling almost 80 hectares of production and had just finished a new, fourth farm, Ayana, in Mau Narok at 2600 meters above sea level. Their four farms—Salgaa (1950 meters above sea level), Turi, and Akina (around 2300 meters above sea level)—were approximately a 40-minute drive from each other, depending on the order you visited them. ( *see pictures at https://www.yulygrosman.com/book)*

Oh man!

*Today is 2025, and our four-year-old son, born in Kenya, likes to say "Oh man!" about everything. Sometimes he says it accurately and to the point, but in many cases, he misses it. Writing for you about those farms and their location, I couldn't hold it back. Oh man! They're such beautiful places there, almost like paradise. I even considered buying land there, but security-wise, I wasn't sure.*

From Salgaa, Girish, whom I had briefly met a few years ago when I opened the Ultra Flo company, took me to his new farm, Ayana. Upon arrival, there were only a few greenhouses with ready production, a temporary packing house that looked like a tractor workshop, and a cold room made from a shipping container. But the roses I saw there! They were amazing. The head size wasn't that big, but the quality—how strong the stems were, how rich the color of the flowers—was breathtaking. I think I lost my ability to speak. In security, and especially in body guarding, we always talk about how people cannot hide their emotions and feelings; those can be easily recognized if you know what you are looking for. These are skills I teach today in the USA, running my corporate seminars and workshops. Skills that help executives not only recognize microaggressions within employees but also are very useful in business and contract negotiations with potential clients. That day, on the farm, I couldn't hide my feelings, and Girish noticed it.

After lunch at the Akina farm, located in Njoro town—a place that would later become my weekly routine—we visited Turi farm, and Girish drove me back. It was a long drive, and we had many interesting conversations when suddenly Girish asked me: *"Yuly, with all your knowledge and expertise, why are you still working for that Israeli company? Why have you never opened your own?"* I told him: *"Lack of money to invest."* Today, I know that being a child of immigrants, whose friends were also from similar families, we had financial fears, and most of us worked from an early age. We had the wrong friends and socialized with the wrong people. I don't have to repeat what thousands of books have already said: *Your environment influences your success.* Some argue it shapes who you are; I disagree. It doesn't shape who you are because it comes down to how you were raised. I've seen many people who, after connecting with wealthy circles and starting to make money, become bad, arrogant, forget their friends, and even disconnect from their families. My belief is that it has nothing to do with shaping who they are, but rather opening a bottle allows a hidden personality to emerge.

Anyway, I'm a bit off the story. Next, Girish asked me if I would consider relocating from Israel, and would Kenya be one of those places?

*Learned Lesson: Opportunity Knocks When You're Ready*

*Life-changing opportunities often appear when you least expect them, especially after periods of reflection and growth. Being open to new possibilities, even seemingly radical ones like international relocation, is crucial for personal and professional advancement.*

# Chapter 45:
# The Offer – A New Chapter in Kenya

I mentioned earlier that I was burned out and felt stuck working in my company, with a strong desire to leave Israel. At the same time, within just one month, I had received two more proposals to leave my current company and work for someone else. One proposal was to work for an Israeli competitor and open a company in Kenya; the others I will keep out of this book. After meeting the owners and directors of this Israeli company and considering a very attractive financial offer, I was less excited. The reason was the corporate hierarchy and the lack of decision-making freedom I was accustomed to.

If you are like me, you'll understand this: my success depended heavily on autonomy. I needed the freedom to act and decide. I was used to hearing, *"The company needs results—do it,"* not *"Ask permission first."* So, despite the appealing offer, I was hesitant.

Meanwhile, Girish and I continued meeting to discuss business. We explored how a new company, a project that we would establish, could purchase and consolidate flowers from the Fontana Group farms. We also discussed Ayana farm and its strong potential. Eventually, Girish said he would speak with his partners and get back to me.

About a month later, I was enjoying a peaceful morning on my balcony in Kfar Saba, Israel—coffee in hand, listening to the birds—when I received a message from Girish asking if we could have a call. I've always believed that people make time for what they value. Even top executives can find a few minutes if they want to. I called him immediately.

On that call, Girish asked if I would consider relocating and working with them. My answer was yes. He asked me to prepare a business plan outlining cooperation strategy, financials, and a timeline. I agreed, with one condition: though I had no formal contract with my current employer, I would not take a single customer with me. For at least a year, I would not approach or work with anyone who was buying Kenyan roses from my existing company. If I joined Fontana Group, we would start from zero.

My business plan was reviewed and approved within a month or two. A decision was made: I would resign from my position as General Manager/CEO at the Israeli company and as Director of Ultra Flo Kenya. I would relocate with my family to Kenya and build a new company that would both sell Fontana Group flowers and consolidate supply from other farms. I would also advise and help manage Fontana's farms—improving brand presence, visibility, quality, and varietal selection for the Russian market, where Fontana had little representation.

By February, I declined all other proposals, including a generous counter-offer from my then-employer to increase my salary. I committed to resigning. Though the standard notice was one month, I promised to stay for two months. I used that time to train the team and leave clear written instructions on strategy and job roles.

There were rumors in the market that I had left on bad terms, but I want to clarify two things. First, I continued supporting and assisting with information and guidance for years after I left. Second, I still occasionally connect with the company's owner to this day.

Just before I left, I led one final impactful project: the Gypsophila project. It was a meaningful way to close that chapter of my life.

## Key Takeaways from Part II

I hope you learned from Part II about how to think strategically, what risks to consider, and how to use critical thinking in global business. After we signed the growing contract with Subati, things progressed well. We were supplying flowers, developing Ultra Flo Kenya, and building a company from the ground up.

The 2008 recession had impacted all markets, including Russia. Our spray roses project was well-timed and successful. Around 2011, I also saw a growing trend: a market shift toward shorter, cheaper roses—but now with bigger heads. We had come full circle, but this time, with better timing and better flowers.

## Reflection and Wrap-up:

**Strategic decisions aren't only about jumping at shiny opportunities. They're about evaluating fit, values, autonomy, and timing. Knowing yourself and what you need to thrive is one of the most underrated leadership skills. Sometimes, walking away from something familiar is the only way to grow into something extraordinary. The chapter that followed was full of risk, challenge, and reward—and it began with the courage to say yes, and the discipline to start clean. What aspects of strategic decision-making in a competitive, global market would you like to explore further, based on these experiences?**

# Part III: Once upon a time, or Business Continuity Management

Chapter 46:

# Perfecto or Just Gypsophila – The Subtle Art of Baby's Breath

## Understanding Gypsophila: More Than Just a Filler

You've likely seen Gypsophila—better known as baby's breath—in countless flower arrangements. Those tiny white "snowflake" blossoms, often seen as mere fillers, actually represent a sophisticated and highly competitive segment of the flower industry.

When I entered the flower business, there were only a few dominant varieties: Gypsophila Million Star (small flowers), and Gypsophila Perfecto (larger, ball-like flowers). Later came Mirabella, visually similar to Perfecto, but with subtly higher flower placement along the stem and a whiter hue—key details for florists and designers.

Why? Because florists might use different stem parts for different bouquet styles. Shorter side branches could be used for compact table arrangements, while longer stems fit taller bouquets. The market's nuanced demand meant even small varietal differences mattered greatly.

## From Field to Cold Room: The Journey of Gypsophila

Gypsophila is typically grown in open fields or simple greenhouses—not as tightly controlled as those used for roses. Once harvested, stems are sorted, treated with a solution, and taken to an "Opening Room," where warmth encourages the flowers to open, much like popcorn in a microwave. After opening, the stems are moved into a cold room, chilled to 4°C, and packed for shipment.

But this is where things get tricky.

Heat is the mortal enemy of Gypsophila. Once "awakened," it can emit surprising levels of heat. I once opened a box where the internal temperature had reached 45°C (113°F). There's even a story—one I believe—about an airport worker in Holland suffering face burns after opening an overheated Gypsophila box. Personally, I've felt the near-scorching heat from such boxes myself.

Whiteflies and other pests added to the challenges. These issues—and the complexity of sanitary regulations—eventually ended our exports to the U.S. and cut into our Australia business.

### Intellectual Property and Legal Turf Wars

Another layer to this market? Intense intellectual property disputes. Danziger, a leading Israeli breeder, enforced its patents aggressively. Growers caught cultivating certain types of Gypsophila without paying royalties were often hit with legal action. For a while, every competitor who dared release a similar product faced immediate litigation.

New varieties, including pink-tinted versions targeting the Japanese market, began to emerge. But sourcing reliable growers remained a challenge. "Reliable" didn't just mean quality; it meant trustworthiness and consistency. Only about 2.5 months of the year had lower demand—otherwise, the market was constantly short on supply.

## Kenya, Israel, and the 60-Gram Standard

I explored growing Gypsophila in Ethiopia with mixed success. I even considered co-investing with Kenyan growers, but conversations led nowhere—until much later. Eventually, I convinced Girish, whose farms produced Gypsophila that rivaled even Israel's best.

Markets like Russia demanded 60-gram, 60cm stems—especially for Mirabella and Perfecto. Million Star only required 40 grams. While Kenya grew Gypsophila, its growers rarely reached those weight standards. One big reason? Kenya removed many of the green leaves to comply with strict pest regulations in Holland and Australia, which lowered stem weight. Israeli growers left those leaves on, making their product heavier and more marketable.

You may now be thinking: *"Why not just train Kenyan growers to leave the leaves on?"* I had the same thought. But behind every action, there are reasons. Leaf removal helped reduce pest risks, especially important when pesticides were limited and expensive.

## A Strategic Growing Agreement

Over time, I identified a grower who showed the consistency and reliability I needed. I proposed a growing contract—similar to those I'd used in Kenya—and helped design the agreement. Though I left my Israeli company before the first flowers from this partnership reached the market, I took pride in laying the groundwork for that success.

## Reflection and Wrap-up:

**Gypsophila isn't just a filler flower—it's a masterclass in niche market dynamics, intellectual property battles, and international logistics. Even the smallest product can carry tremendous risk, strategy, and reward.**

**Sometimes, a "small" side project becomes a final triumph in a chapter of your life. For me, Gypsophila symbolized**

everything I'd learned about precision, partnership, and persistence in the flower business.

As I prepared for my next big move—to Kenya and a new life—I allowed myself 1.5 months of rest. A reset. A rare and necessary gift I now recommend to every high-performing professional: take time to reflect before the next sprint.

# Chapter 47:

# My Home in Kenya – A New Chapter, A Fated Meeting

## The Relocation: A Project in Itself

May 2012. I moved to Kenya with my family and an unexpected companion: an Irish Wolfhound. Two years earlier, I had bought him in Russia as a three-month-old puppy and brought him to Israel. At just three months, Fenrir weighed 18kg (nearly 40 lbs) according to the airline scales and ticket – quite a notable companion!

Relocation is a separate project by itself, demanding meticulous planning, preparation, and strategy. This isn't just because it profoundly affects your family, but also because it impacts business timelines, strategy, and overall success if executed poorly. I had partially gained this experience when opening the Ultra Flo company – navigating company registration, work permits, licenses, office setup, and logistics. This time, it wasn't as hard. Today, I advise investors and startups on such projects, guiding them through opening branches or registering companies and moving teams from abroad. My focus is on making the process smooth, identifying risk factors, and developing effective mitigation strategies.

The next couple of months were a whirlwind of organizing logistics, informing the market about my move, and meticulously choosing the varieties we would grow across Girish's farms, which now boasted 100 hectares in production. It was pretty much similar to what I had done before. The crucial nuance this time was my strategic targeting of the upcoming Moscow Flower Expo in September 2012. I knew this was my chance to secure the first new clients, setting the stage for a strong push towards International Women's Day on March 8th, 2013. I anticipated markets would struggle with flower shortages, and demand would be high. With four farms and 100 hectares of flowers, it was an immense opportunity!

## A Love Story Unfolding: The Unseen Connection

I must pause here and take you, my readers, back to the beginning of this book where I wrote about my future wife. Just to remind you, read it again:

*Imagine: Living 500 meters from your future wife, never meeting. Five years pass; she photos your number from a poster but never calls. Over seven years later, amidst the tragedy of a terrorist attack where someone was killed, she finally calls you for security training. That call? It sparked an amazing love story and led to a child raised in happiness and love.*

I think this is the perfect place, the right chapter, to elaborate on it. Life isn't always perfect; people get married and sometimes get divorced. I am not the type of person who writes books or coaches leveraging bad past experiences—portraying a spouse as "bad" or a "monster"—and then detailing what was learned from that part of life and how things are now "great." I believe that from every relationship, we learn something and hopefully become better and more ready for the next one. The same applied in my case. I have great and beautiful twin girls from my first marriage. Somewhere along the way, things went wrong between me and my ex-wife. Both of us made mistakes; in some cases, people just don't match and keep enduring it until they can no longer.

Back then in 2012, things were good between us. We lived in Nairobi that first year. I had long hair, wore a piercing in my ear, and walked the only Irish Wolfhound in Nairobi. Trust me, it was something very notable; it was hard to miss. Three to four times a week, I would leave early in the morning, around 5 AM, heading toward our farms, a four-hour drive each direction. I'd return late in the evening after visiting many farms, teaching and training people on what needed to be done, and building relationships with the farm managers. In total, back then, I think there were more than 3,000 people across the four farms. This is when I truly started to appreciate having a personal driver.

But the story is different. At the exact same time, just 500 meters from our home (an apartment, before I moved to a house), there was a woman, a girl I would say. A girl who was born in New Jersey, USA, spent years in San Francisco, and around the same time, in 2012, started a company with her business partner. A company with many branches, including Latin America, that connected investors in the Impact Investing scene with startups in emerging markets.

*Learned Lesson:*

*Relocating isn't just about logistics—it's about mindset. Every move is a pivot point, and how you handle the transition will define your next chapter. Whether it's work, family, or falling in love—be fully present.*

## Reflection and Wrap Up

In my early days in Kenya, I was setting up a new business, adapting to a new culture, and unknowingly living a block away from my future partner in life and work. Life unfolds in beautiful, unexpected ways—often when you are too busy to notice.

Sometimes, a relocation isn't just a move—it's a reboot. You never know what opportunities or people might be around the corner. Stay open. Stay curious. Build your life the same way you'd build a new company: step by step, but with a big vision in mind.

**Near Misses: The "Adjustment Bureau" in Real Life**

Every morning and evening, that girl was walking to her office, meetings, and the nearby Junction Mall—the same road I walked with my huge puppy, Fenrir, who stood taller than me when upright. And trust me, I am not a short person. But back then, I had my life, and she had hers. We didn't meet; we didn't even look at each other. Our lives weren't ready to cross yet.

Have you ever seen the movie *The Adjustment Bureau* by George Nolfi? I believe that movie is about us.

*The Adjustment Bureau* is a 2011 American science fiction romantic thriller film starring Matt Damon and Emily Blunt, loosely based on the Philip K. Dick short story "Adjustment Team."

The movie follows David Norris (Matt Damon), a charismatic politician on the brink of winning a U.S. Senate seat. His life takes an unexpected turn when he has a chance encounter with Elise Sellas (Emily Blunt), a beautiful and free-spirited contemporary dancer. They share an undeniable connection, but their burgeoning relationship is immediately thwarted by mysterious men in hats.

These men are agents of the enigmatic "Adjustment Bureau," a powerful organization that intervenes in people's lives to ensure events unfold according to a predetermined "Plan" created by a higher power known as "The Chairman."

David accidentally glimpses the Bureau's work and learns that his destiny, and that of Elise, are not meant to intertwine according to the Plan.

The Bureau agents explain that allowing David and Elise to be together would derail both of their predetermined paths to greatness—David is meant to become President, and Elise a world-renowned dancer and choreographer. Despite the Bureau's considerable power and efforts to keep them apart, David and Elise fight against fate itself, risking everything to be together and pursue their own free will.

The film explores themes of destiny versus free will, the nature of choice, and the idea of a guiding force or plan shaping human lives. It's a thrilling chase across New York City as David and Elise try to outrun the agents and ultimately seek to confront the Chairman to plead for their right to choose their own future.

The second time we almost crossed paths was in 2015. During that time, I was still in the flower business and had already established my martial arts school—which I would also describe as an entrepreneurial journey. It's a business in itself, with its own strategy, branding, marketing, and growth. By the end of 2014, I had made a decision, based on market research and analysis, that there wasn't a single truly professional martial arts school in all of Kenya. I was already a 1st Dan Black Belt in Shotokan Karate and, I would say, almost a brown belt in Kyokushin from Israel. Perhaps a few words about that.

I started my martial arts journey just a year after we moved from the USSR to Israel. The boiling aggression towards me—us repatriants from the USSR—pushed me into it. Between and after school and work, I trained, I would say very professionally, in Kyokushin in Israel. The system, called Seido, was founded by Tadashi Nakamura, who lives in the USA. It was a combative version of Karate. Our school was great!

Sensei Eli Bitran, who ran his school in Ra'anana, Israel, in a bank building basement, did a great job. Besides teaching us, his students, values and respect, his investment was in basics, passion, and fundamentals. I trained there from age 12.5 until joining the IDF at age 18.5. I was supposed to have my exams for a brown belt, Kyu 2, when I joined the IDF. His approach was one of discovery, and in addition to Karate, we studied Aikido and Krav Maga, which back then was not as popular as today.

Unfortunately, after the IDF, I couldn't get back to classes as I finished my service as a Disabled Veteran with several major surgeries. It is a long story that I don't like to share, but at the same time, I'm proud of it, because immediately after my first surgery, when I opened my eyes waking up from anesthesia, the very first question I asked my doctor was if I would be able to go back to martial arts. His answer was that I should pray and work hard not to be in a wheelchair at some point. I told him in Russian, "F***k you," and by 2023, I was holding a 1st Dan Black Belt in Shotokan Karate, a 3rd Dan Black Belt Shadow Krav Maga International Instructor, a 3rd Dan Black Belt Shadow Jitsu, and a Bodyguard Instructor. In addition, I had seven martial arts schools in Kenya, training civilians, special forces, police, and corporate clients.

This is the first time I publicly admit that I was also addicted to painkillers for many years, such as OxyContin, Oxycodone, and many others prescribed to me by doctors and supplied by the Rehabilitation Department of the IDF. I also had two major surgeries related to my disability and at least five more related to the consequences of that. I am proud of all that, because if I managed to do what I do and did in my life, You Can Too!

I quit smoking and quit painkillers by myself, without any formal treatment. Pain, I learned to live with. It is my constant companion. Sometimes, worse, and sometimes not so bad. But. I manage.

Now, back to the story. After opening a martial arts school in Kenya, in the same style I used to train in, with values, respect, no delays, or using a phone to bring in business, one strategy was putting my posters around the expat community's places. One of those posters was found by my future wife in one of the farmers' markets. She took a picture because she had done Krav Maga in New York, but she never called me. At least not back then, in 2015. So, it was the second time when we didn't meet.

*Learned Lesson:*

*Resilience isn't forged in comfort. It's built through facing pain, adversity, and inner battles—and still choosing to move forward. Whether you're building a business, healing a body, or searching for love, your future often hinges on how well you endure the trials that precede it.*

**Reflection and Wrap-up:**

**Sometimes, we're not meant to meet someone until we've walked the hard path that prepares us for them. These near misses are life's way of saying, "Not yet—but soon."**

**Fate has its timeline. Your job is to keep showing up, doing the work, and growing into the person your future demands. Love, health, and purpose may not arrive when you want—but they often arrive exactly when you're finally ready.**

# Chapter 48:
# The Outer Security Circle: A Tragic Premonition

Between 2015 and 2019, the flower business went down due to many factors that I will share later, as I believe it's critical for you to know how to navigate such global changes. In 2018, I completely stopped exporting flowers and began working as a consultant and advisor. Simultaneously, I restarted my security and training business.

Now days, when advising businesses on their strategy, I draw heavily on my experience from both business and security/bodyguarding. In top-level security, we have a term: Outer Security Circle. To make it simple, imagine your office building. The security guards, CCTV, and alarms you have are your Inner Circle. A few blocks away from it is an Outer Circle. It is a space from where you have enough time to prevent, plan, and respond. This is where it's not too late.

Part of my security services involved providing Security Penetration Tests to clients. This is where a company hires me to find a way to gain unauthorized access or to create a situation where a major physical disruption, such as a terrorist attack or a robbery, could occur.

Sometimes it takes time to prepare—days, weeks, even months. This includes surveillance, gap detection, and a detailed plan of how I will get inside or complete my mission without being discovered. At the end, I would provide a report with recommendations on what and how to improve.

Sometimes, to gain attention and a new client, I would conduct an individual security penetration test. The business complex and the Dusit D2 Hotel, located at 14 Riverside Drive, Nairobi, Kenya, was one of them. The first time I conducted a basic security penetration test was in October 2015. Without going into details, after and without any prior preparations, I managed to pass through the hotel security. I then requested a meeting with the head of security and the general manager of the hotel. I remember the meeting very well. After highlighting the security gaps and discussing possible training and improvements, we had a few more meetings.

Unfortunately, Kenya is a country with a "Hakuna Matata" mentality, and the perception of security is often very poor. Corporations are reluctant to improve and invest, often, I believe, due to two main factors:

One is the society itself. The public or clients, if you prefer, allow them to do so. They don't care about security;

they don't demand better security, so public places don't want to spend on it.

The second reason is insurance and licensing. There is no demand by insurance companies with clear instructions on what security should look like at a facility, and how it should work and advance. For example, in Israel, it would be almost impossible to get an operating license for a public place without an insurance policy that demands specific security standards as well.

I can assume that some of my readers might accuse me of some kind of revenge for putting this chapter down. I am not going to argue about that, but people who know me well would disagree with you.

The hotel management and the head of security refused the training despite a very strong case and significant gaps exposed by the basic penetration test I conducted. Why am I telling you that? Because there is a direct link between this, a tragic event, and how I met my future wife.

In 2017, I was hired as an external security consultant and advisor, helping a security company in Kenya improve operations and propose business strategies on becoming the best provider in the market among competitors. I was hired for three months, but the company extended this contract for three years. The security company provided three market solutions: security guard services, ERT (Emergency Response Team)—this was the department I was handling and improving—and country-wide logistics services.

Destiny is a wired thing; many do not believe in that. But it happened that the same complex on 14 Riverside Drive were clients of the security company I was advising. The security market in Kenya was properly divided between several main operators: G4S, KK Security (which was later acquired by Garda World), Wells Fargo Kenya, and the rest were much smaller. I worked with many of them, and I managed to piss off most of them. That significantly increased the threat list on my life from when I was working as security in Israel. Every time a corporation hired me to do a security penetration test, one of those companies, and sometimes all of them, would receive warning letters from their clients based on my security gaps reports. The same happened with 14 Riverside. At least three different companies were securing that space and the hotel. The company I was consulting was securing the main entrance to the entire complex, some office buildings, and providing the ERT. Every time someone pressed a panic button or an alarm was triggered, the ERT team would arrive.

Despite the guarding department not being part of my contract, I submitted many reports highlighting security issues, such as sleeping guards. The type of contract I had allowed me flexibility, and at some point, as a business strategy, I offered the security company a new approach: they would provide free security penetration tests, conducted by me, to their corporate clients. This would improve security services and, at the same time, save money for clients who were hiring such services from a third party. During one of the board meetings we had, I was informed that the management of Riverside 14 had refused such a service.

*Learned Lesson:*

*Your warnings may not always be heard. But your responsibility is not to silence them—it is to speak up, prepare, and keep raising the standard. Security isn't just a service; it's foresight in action.*

**Reflection and Wrap-up:**

**Often, what separates tragedy from triumph is one decision—taken or ignored—weeks or even years before. What looks like over-preparation in peace often proves to be lifesaving when crisis hits.**

**Don't wait until disaster knocks to ask the right questions. Build your Outer Security Circle now—in your business, your life, your relationships. The time to act is before the threat is near.**

# Chapter 49:

# The Attack That Took Lives, The Call That Forged a New One

January 15, 2019: A Day Etched in Memory

I remember that day vividly.

**January 15, 2019, 08:30 AM:**

Instead of heading directly to my office (provided by the security company I was advising), I made a random visit to Two Rivers Mall, located on the other side of town, not far from the well-known Village Market Mall, the U.S. Embassy, and the UN Headquarters in Kenya. After meeting with managers at a few banks—clients where our company provided ERT (Emergency Response Team) services—we agreed to run a test to evaluate our team's performance. This would allow me to identify and improve gaps in security, response, and customer service. I hope you'll understand why I won't expose all the details.

**10:00 AM:**

Based on my instructions, the bank managers triggered several alarms. I received notifications from the Alarm Control Room manager that all alarms were well-received, and the designated team was dispatched.

**11:00 AM:**

I arrived at another customer, a well-known law office. My purpose was essentially the same: to conduct a test and address a specific complaint they had from a week prior.

**1:10 PM:**

After a few more meetings, I finally arrived at my office. I used my Control Room access badge to open a heavy, bulletproof door. Based on my previous report, this door made no sense in terms of security; some of the surrounding walls weren't strong enough to stop bullets, and the door itself actually created a death trap for anyone inside.

After checking the Control Room and retrieving reports, I made a call to the guarding department, even though it wasn't part of my contract. Like you, I believe that knowledge must be used whenever possible. After getting an update about broken ERT cars and their repair status, it was almost past 2 PM when I finally got my coffee and opened my laptop.

**2:30 PM:**

I wasn't called by the Control Room, but listening to the radio, I heard something about shooting and an explosion in the city. Simultaneously, I started receiving updates from my personal security channels about a possible terrorist attack at 14 Riverside Drive, Nairobi.

I ran into the Control Room, but no one knew what to do. More disturbingly, there were no updates from the field. What happened next was an absolute flashback to my time working security in Israel during the Second Intifada. Years of that environment—terrorist attacks, threats, and procedures—had built a resilience and knowledge you can't learn from books.

I was always known as someone good at multitasking, but I didn't know a person could perform so many tasks at once. I was also quite far from the physical attack—our offices were about 9km (5 miles) away. From my experience, I knew there was no point in rushing to the site. I needed to be in the Control Room.

As mentioned earlier, the company provided guarding services to the complex, including guards at the main entrance, and the ERT. I knew there had been no alarms from that place for the last two hours, meaning no one from our ERT should have been there. Fortunately, our teams used radio for communication, because in many countries during such situations, authorities shut down mobile connectivity to reduce the risk of a secondary explosive attack and to prevent communication among attackers.

The guarding department was in total disarray. No one could clearly tell me who the guards on duty were, their physical location as per the shift roster, and where they were after the attack. I needed this information, not just for human factors, but for operational reasons to support authorities.

21 people were killed in this attack. One of them was a U.S. citizen, a global entrepreneur, a Facebook contact I never met: Jason Spindler. My son's middle name is Jason.

## Destiny's Kiss: The VIP Survival Course

That tragedy, and the "Plan" created by a higher power—almost like in the Adjustment Bureau movie I referenced earlier—brought my future wife and me together.

A month later, I received a message from a woman asking for security training. Her name was Patricia.

She was very cautious and initially refused to meet. She asked endless questions about my work and references. I sent her testimonials, certificates, and background details. At the same time, I started receiving messages from past clients—Patricia had contacted them, asking for feedback.

*I know you are waiting for the Kiss moment. It is there.*

Eventually, I believe it was Andres—a client, expat, and lawyer at the International Criminal Court—who convinced her. His reference letter read:

RECOMMENDATION LETTER

*To Whom it May Concern:*

*I would like to offer my highest recommendation for the V.I.P. Survival Course taught by instructor Yuly Grosman of Sacura Martial Arts Academy. I completed this course in 2016 while I was based in Nairobi, Kenya. I chose to take this course because my work frequently sends me to hostile environments, and I wanted advanced situational awareness and self-defense training beyond what is offered by standard HEAT (Hostile Environment Awareness Training) courses.*

*The course was excellent. Yuly provides no-nonsense, intense training that demands full commitment. It is very physical and highly realistic. Expect to come home sore and bruised, but confident.*

*Yuly was flexible, frequently traveling to my home to accommodate my schedule. I recommend this course to anyone willing to accept physical and psychological challenge to improve their survival in hostile environments.*

*Please feel free to contact me for more insight: andresxxxxxx@gmail.com*

At the time, my personal life was strained. Living under the same roof doesn't always mean being in a relationship.

After meeting Patricia, we structured 25 hours of intensive training within a month. Simultaneously, I was training two other clients and consulting.

Patricia shared her story. Her business partner had been killed in the attack. All her staff had been present during it. She was planning to return to the U.S.

I'll admit, at some point during this training, I became emotionally involved. But I remained professional. I was the instructor; she was the client.

## The Roof Session: Where Training Met Fate

The course included real-life scenarios: contact combat, awareness, communication, knife fighting, and improvised weapons. One session took place in a kitchen— we broke a mug, a wedding gift, .during a defense drill.

She was living with a just married couple who were friends and we used their apartment for training

She also trained at the shooting range with real firearms under my supervision.

When friends ask us about our first date, we say: she was running in forests, shooting a 9mm, and fighting off chokeholds.

The final session took place on the rooftop of a Nairobi apartment. After a pool training exercise, I handed her a towel and told her, "The course is complete."

Then came the kiss.

Shortly after, she told me she might be leaving Kenya.

That summer, after my ex-wife and kids returned to Israel, Patricia and I reconnected.

**Learned Lesson:**

*Tragedy rearranges lives. Out of unimaginable loss can emerge unexpected new beginnings. But only if you stay open to the next mission, even while healing from the last.*

**Reflection and Wrap-up:**

You don't always know which encounter will change your life. Sometimes, it's a referral. Sometimes, it starts with a training session. Sometimes, it starts after an explosion.

What life-altering events are preparing you for something greater—even if you can't see it yet? Stay alert. Stay available. Stay human.

# Chapter 50:
# Nairobi 2012 – The Art of Standing Out

## The "What Stands Out" Mindset: From Security to Business

Promising that this book is not just about me, but a roadmap based on experience for how you can build your business, improve operations, and navigate uncertainty, I should take you back to 2012, when I had just moved to Kenya.

I've already mentioned that by 2012, competition had intensified, and new approaches were desperately needed. There was a requirement to create something extraordinary, something that would instantly stand out and be well-recognized in the market.

In VIP security and bodyguard courses, we employ a method called *"what stands out."* This is a mindset I've frequently used—and successfully applied—later when founding a food production business.

## What is the "What Stands Out" Mindset?

Let me give you two examples, one from security and one from your own everyday life.

### Security Example

Set the book down for a moment, close your eyes, and imagine this:

*You're walking in a central city—maybe somewhere in Europe or New York. Your child or loved one is walking just ahead of you. It's a sunny spring day, 20°C (70°F), with a light breeze. Then you get a mysterious message: someone on this very street is planning a terrorist attack. No names. No photos. Just that message.*

*Your adrenaline spikes. You scan the crowd. You're no longer simply walking—you're analyzing, urgently. Who doesn't belong? Who stands out? Someone overdressed for the weather? Someone sweatig or unusually calm? Twitchy? Frozen? Masked in emotion?*

*You're reading posture, clothing, micro-expressions. You're in survival mode, scanning for the anomaly—the one person who doesn't fit the environment.*

That is the art of spotting what stands out.

## Business Example

You're building a brand. Let's say you're producing a revolutionary new yogurt: organic, sustainable, preservative-free, female-led production team. Fantastic product. But here's the rub: *if they can't see it, they can't buy it.*

Here's your exercise:

*Go to a major grocery store. Head to the dairy aisle. Back up a few feet. Let your eyes scan the yogurt wall. Hundreds of options. Now—close your eyes. Clear your mind. Open them again.*

*Which one product instantly grabs your attention?*

*Not because you've bought it before. Not because of price. But because it stands out.*

*That's the one. That's the strategy.*

## From Yogurt to Flowers

Before delivering premium flowers into a market overflowing with thousands of packages, I had to make sure *my* box stood out. Think Costco-sized flower warehouses. Hundreds of thousands of flower bunches. Each one shouting for attention.

My product had to be:

- Visually different
- Memorably packaged

- Emotionally resonant

The client didn't have time to inspect every stem. They made subconscious judgments within seconds.

**What stood out won.**

*Learned Lesson:*

*Whether in a crisis or a crowded market, the ability to detect—or be—the thing that stands out determines your success. Standing out is not a gimmick. It's a strategy.*

**Reflection and Wrap-up:**

**Whether you're protecting lives or launching a product, the question remains the same:** *Can you be noticed when it matters most?* **What makes you—and your offering—distinct in a sea of sameness?**

**Don't blend in. In business, as in life and security, invisibility is dangerous. Make deliberate choices to be visible, memorable, and unmistakable. Build with boldness.**

**What about you? Next time you launch something—whether it's a pitch, a product, or a personal brand—step back and ask:** *What makes it stand out?*

# Chapter 51:
# Brand Strategy: Naming and Packaging for Impact

## MAO Flowers Ltd.: The Power of a Memorable Name

First, a company name that's easy to remember and stands out.

What do you know about Mao Zedong? Yes, I'm talking about the Chinese politician. In different countries, he's perceived differently—mostly not in a good way, especially in Europe, Russia, and the West. In Russia, almost every adult has heard this name. How is he related to my company? Zero. But I named my company MAO Flowers Ltd!

MAO stands for Main Africa Operator Flowers Ltd. But what people remembered and talked about was this:

*"Hey, I saw amazing flowers from Kenya last week at my competitor's warehouse. I can't remember the company name. Do you?"*

*"Yes, I do! It was something about that Chinese dictator... MAO or something..."*

Friends told me I was crazy to name the company MAO. Many times. But do you know how easily that name was remembered in the markets? Almost always. Do you know how many of those friends and advisors actually built something memorable or entrepreneurial? Maybe 10%.

## From Naming to Packaging: The Complete Brand Experience

After finalizing the name and registering the company, I dove into the next essential layer of strategy: packaging.

Think of it like peeling an orange: you start from the outside and move inward to the seeds. Your product might be great, but without the right visual and functional presentation, it won't survive first impressions—or transit.

Back then, I was still working closely with packaging producers. After several rounds of trial and error—including importing new types of paper—we finally developed a strong, color-accurate flower box. Durable, functional, and visually distinct.

But the box was only the beginning.

The next critical layer: the sleeve.

Not a shirt sleeve—but the plastic cellophane layer you see on bunches of flowers. Not the decorative one from a flower shop, but the industrial one used during transport and the other is SFK.

There are different types of sleeves, but all are needed to do five things:

- Protect the flowers during shipment

- Extend shelf life

- Reduce moisture absorption (to avoid botrytis)

- Be cost-effective

- Visually stand out

**Reverse-Engineering Shelf Appeal**

In 2012, no one in Kenya had yet cracked this kind of sleeve. The only quality version I had seen was from Ecuador—light but water-resistant, non-absorbent, with high-end printed graphics.

On my next trip to Europe and Russia, I collected 15–20 of the best sleeves I could find from flower markets. I laid them out on the floor of my office, comparing materials, design, and print. Then I took them home.

Why? To simulate a more distracting environment—like the chaos of a flower warehouse.

Eventually, I took it even further.

I created mock-ups: fake flower bunches placed in real baskets. I built a simulated environment to replicate my customer's reality.

Only then did I finalize the size, shape, color, and design of the MAO sleeve.Bear with me, in the next chapter you will learn about SFK.

### Learned Lesson: The Power of Strategic Differentiation

*To succeed in a crowded market, you must deliberately differentiate—from your brand name to your packaging and beyond. Don't just follow trends. Study your environment, simulate your customer's experience, and engineer every detail to stand out.*

### Reflection and Wrap-up:

Too many entrepreneurs focus only on the product. But your customer first sees your *presentation*. What catches the eye opens the door. What's inside must deliver.

In a saturated market, visibility is the gateway to value. Make bold, thoughtful choices—ones that trigger curiosity, recognition, and action.

Your next move: Revisit your brand. What are people really remembering about you? What's standing out?

# Chapter 52:
# The Final Touch – Branding, Strategy, and ROI

## The Last Mile: Ensuring Customer Delight

The last touch. When your client is satisfied, it's good; when they're happy and satisfied, it's even better. Today, it's common that when you buy a flower bouquet, the salesperson attaches a small sachet with powder. You add that powder to water, and it increases, or at least should increase, your flowers' vase life.

I already knew that many companies used poor quality powder, so I ordered samples from five different companies available in the market and conducted numerous trials. Finally, my brand, the entire "Orange," was ready and packed.

Ultimately, the MAO Flowers Ltd. perfect branding was ready. Of course, it took time, and I couldn't wait for all components to be ready simultaneously. But the first look—the boxes and improved, plain SFK (Specialized Flower Keeper) with sleeves—were ready in a few months, just before the September 2012 International Flowers Expo.

### The "Look. Listen. Respond." Philosophy: A Guiding Principle

If you remember, from the beginning of this book, I was explaining how everything is connected. This holds true in all businesses, and especially in flowers, simply because it's a sensitive, short-term live product. Planning in every business is essential, just as it is in security, VIP protection, and other aspects of life.

While writing this chapter, I published a post on my LinkedIn Newsletter titled:

"Remember *The Bodyguard* with Kevin Costner & Whitney Houston?"

The post explores:

> **What does The Bodyguard have to do with executive leadership? More than you think.**

Because in today's volatile world, it's not always the obvious threats that break us — *it's the ones we never saw coming.*

In this article, I share the mindset I teach to both bodyguards and CEOs: "LOOK. LISTEN. RESPOND." Not just in life-or-death moments… but in boardrooms, burnout, and team dynamics where reputation, performance, and trust are always on the line.

If you rely on baby gates, airbags, health benefits, or HR to keep you safe — this might be the most important leadership article you read today.

You can find this and many other articles and posts on my page or website, www.yulygrosman.com.

## Backwards Planning: The Road to ROI

Even before moving to Kenya, I already had a business plan with its implementation strategies and timeline. While generally, I do admire the Gantt Chart, in Kenya, it's hard to use because of the pervasive "Hakuna Matata" attitude. That doesn't mean I wasn't pushing and wasn't fast. I certainly had the Gantt chart in my head and was trying to be even ahead of it. My planning started from the goal backward instead of moving forward.

The goal was market sales, ROI (Return on Investment), recognition, and growth. In flowers, this also heavily depends on holidays. I knew that my branding wouldn't be fully ready for the September 1st holiday, but I also knew that having a full brand by mid-September 2012 would attract clients who were already targeting the 2013 Women's Day.

This meant planning in advance, looking for trusted suppliers. My name was more than well-known in the markets. So, my calculations began from March 8th, 2013, and worked backward to June 2012, when I had just relocated to Kenya and started MAO Flowers Ltd. Shipments for September 1st would usually start around August 18th from Kenya, meaning orders would be placed somewhere around August 1st. I had only two months to launch the company. This included company registration, shareholders, bank accounts, export licenses, an office (preferably at the airport), packaging material, and much more.

Simultaneously, I was preparing for the Moscow Flower Expo: booking space, designing graphic and advertisement materials, arranging hotels and flight tickets, shipping flower samples, sourcing gifts for clients (something authentically African; the Maasai Market with its souvenirs had been incredibly helpful for years), printing business cards, hiring models to assist in our stand, and planning money collection processes, etc.

As I just mentioned, all of this had to be ready early enough. If successful, we would have clients already in October, which would significantly increase sales in January for Women's Day.

It was a difficult, yet interesting time. Again, I was building something. I love the creation process; I love successful creations. My motto is: There are no failures. From every mistake, you learn and get better. From every dead-end, you step aside and find more ways to exist.

Remember this!

The majority of people plan, review, then act.

It's called 40:40:20 (40% plan, 40% review, 20% act). But you should do 10% plan, 80% do, and 10% review.

It took me 1.5 years from the moment we relocated to Kenya to achieve a full ROI! Just think about it: my relocation package, company establishment, Operational Expenses (OPEX), and Capital Expenditures (CAPEX)—in a year and a half, I brought the company balance to ZERO.

### Learned Lesson: Strategic Execution and Rapid ROI

*Aggressive, backward-engineered planning, coupled with a bias for action (10% plan, 80% do, 10% review), is crucial for rapid market penetration and achieving quick Return on Investment, especially in fast-paced or competitive industries. A strong, memorable brand—even a controversial one—can significantly aid market recognition.*

Reflection and Wrap-up:

You can't afford to wait for everything to be perfect. Launch early, refine fast, and stay focused on the end goal. In a time-sensitive industry, speed and visibility are your biggest assets.

Be bold in your vision. Plan from the outcome backward. The sooner you're in the market, the faster you can learn, adapt, and scale. And remember—no one remembers the safe brand; they remember the one that made them look twice.

Your next move: Map out your goals, then reverse-engineer the path. Where do you start *if* you already knew you'd succeed?

# Chapter 53: Goals Achieved, New Horizons Beckon

## Settling into Nairobi: A City in Flux

Goal achievements do not mean there are no more goals. The trip to Moscow was great, and perhaps needs its own chapter. But for now, we should outline the goals and what was achieved. My relocation to Kenya was complete. For the first week, we lived in the same apartment building I had used for the last five years every time I visited Kenya: Salonika Villas, located centrally in Lavington, just between two major malls, The Junction Mall and the Yaya Center. Both were popular among expats. *(see pictures at https://www.yulygrosman.com/book)*

To clarify, when I first came to Kenya in 2006, there were only four or five major malls: The Junction Mall (which I'll call the "old Junction"), the Yaya Center (quite old but expensive and owned by Israelis), the Sarit Centre in Westlands, the Village Market next to the UN and the USA Embassy, and the Westgate. The last one was also tragically targeted in a terrorist attack in 2013; that day, I was supposed to be there with my kids, but was tired after all my trips to farms and decided to rest.

That's pretty much all there was, but by 2012, when I relocated to Kenya, and until 2023, when we moved to the USA, all the old malls were renovated, and countless new ones were built. To emphasize how Nairobi developed and became an international hub, here's a story about how I made a stupid miscalculation of an opportunity.

Between 2006, when I first came, and 2010, you could buy an acre of land in central Nairobi for up to USD 10,000. Which, I was offered several times. But back then, I couldn't conceive or imagine that one day I would live in Kenya, and having land would be much less risky for an expat. By 2012, there was almost no one-acre plot of land available for purchase in central Nairobi, and by 2020, the price for such land was above USD 1 million.

I witnessed Nairobi's transformation every year. Many, and in some places even most, private homes around Lavington, Kileleshwa, and Westlands were knocked down and replaced by apartment buildings with gyms, pools, parking, restaurants, and hotels. Every time I came to Nairobi after 2010, I would see that one more amazing restaurant had disappeared, and a new construction project had begun. It was also a time for security changes. If before 2012, people were afraid to walk on streets at night, and even driving felt unsafe, with all car doors and windows closed, after 2014, nightclubs were everywhere, and people drove with almost no fear. Still, walking alone at night isn't entirely safe, but it's much better.

## MAO Flowers: Strategic Choices and Early Triumphs

Back to achievements. Within a week in Salonika, I found a four-bedroom apartment with an SQ (servant quarter)—an apartment of 2,000 sq. ft., located near my future wife's residence.

Girish secured my 4x4 Toyota Surf, big and strong enough for farm travel, hired a driver, registered the company, set up the office, and acquired boxes and other equipment and documents.

I even selected new varieties we should plant. Two of my favorite roses from my selection were Perfume De Grande and Creme De Grande, both by Interplant Breeder. *(see pictures by scanning this QR code)*

Both are beautiful, large-headed (approximately 7cm Hybrid-T) roses carrying an intoxicating perfume scent. One was a soft, delicate pinkish blush, the other a rich, luminous cream. Gathered together, perhaps with only a tender touch of dark green leather fern like shadows against moonlight, these weren't merely flowers. They were a quiet conjuring. A tangible sense of magic bloomed outward from them, the air around alive with luminous freshness, a palpable atmosphere that brought an involuntary smile, like sudden warmth after a chill.

This wasn't a bouquet for obligation, or for display on just any table. This was a language whispered in petals and perfume, meant for the one you carry like a precious, beautiful secret in your heart. For the friend whose soul mirrors yours, the lover who sees your truest light, the one whose love is a treasure, and who, in turn, yearns to be loved with such felt beauty. A gift of pure sensation, wrapped in reverence and the undeniable scent of a love story.

I'll be honest with you: choosing these two was a very brave experiment for me. I wasn't sure, but my gut feeling told me I should select and plant them. So, we did. But just in case, we planted only ¼ of an acre for each. I designated these two varieties as premium in my price list, and customers could only get a limited number of stems. Back then, I don't think anyone else was growing them in Kenya; they were new varieties. Together with those, I selected around four or five Spray Roses, since they were in the highest demand.

The end of 2012 and the beginning of 2013 were great. Women's Day was successful, and we gained many clients. I was constantly moving between farms, leaving home in Nairobi very early, and driving 4-7 hours around different farms, including ours. Every two months, I flew to visit our clients. I can't say I was burned out; I was excited with my new creation. I kept my promise and, for at least the first year, did not approach a single client from the company I used to work for. I know well about all the rumors in the market, but I also know that the owner of the company I was working for came to me at the Moscow Flower Expo asking if I really sent back to him a client (let's call her "L. Client"). I did. In Moscow, many came to my stand asking to work with me; if the client used to buy Kenyan flowers from me when I was running that Israeli company, I would apologize and send them 50 feet left toward the booth of my former company.

Just before Women's Day 2013, two big clients from Ukraine contacted me. This was already a time when competition in Kenya was very big; many export companies had opened, demand for flowers was high, but supply and production for Women's Day were low.

*Learned Lesson: Proactive Planning and Ethical Market Entry*

*Achieving initial goals is a milestone, not an endpoint; continuous goal-setting is vital for sustained growth. Strategic backward planning from major market events (like holidays) enables precise operational execution. Furthermore, maintaining ethical practices and honoring commitments, even in competitive environments, builds long-term trust and a strong reputation within your industry.*

**Reflection and Wrap-up:**

**Big wins come from bold moves—but also from principled ones. Your reputation follows you. The decision to turn away business out of integrity might hurt in the short term, but it lays the foundation for longevity and respect.**

**Don't wait to be ready—move with purpose and adjust along the way. Be clear on your values, plan from the outcome, and never underestimate the compound interest of trust.**

**Your next move:** What's one bold, ethical decision you can make this week that your future self (and business) will thank you for?

# Chapter 54:
# Taxation, Creativity, and the Art of the Loophole

## Taxes: A Test of Creativity and Experience

Did you know that tax payments directly depend on your level of creativity and experience?

Let's do a quick jump back to 2008, when I founded the Kenyan company Ultra Flo Ltd. as a sister company to the Israeli one where I was working as CEO. At the beginning of 2008, I was already involved in most company operations: logistics, finance, payments, and even delving into audit reports without actually having formal finance training.

Later that same year, during our wedding—which I mentioned earlier—the owner of our company suddenly fell unwell and left early. The next day, I was informed he had emergency surgery that resulted in a biopsy revealing cancer. For a few weeks, he was hospitalized, and 100% of his functions were transferred to me. That experience was incredibly helpful. Later, after relocating to Kenya, I was ready to navigate changes. But remember, I mentioned earlier that *knowledge without experience is often not enough.*

Until 2013, in Kenya, there were no VAT taxes on agricultural and horticulture products, especially for the export of such. The MAO Flowers company, besides representing the four Fontana Group farms, was a separate entity and also purchased flowers from other growers. If you are still new in the business field, I'll make it simple.

Imagine you purchase flowers from a local grower for USD 100. Based on the law (before 2013), you would pay the USD 100. Next, you export the flowers, and they leave the country through the necessary channels.

But then, the government came and said you now had to pay 16% VAT on it. So, from now on, that USD 100 became USD 116. The USD 100 went to the farm, and the USD 16 went to the government.

In "normal" countries, such as those in the West, Europe, or the Middle East, when you export goods, by submitting proof of export documents, the government will pay you back the 16%—the USD 16. But Kenya is not a "very normal" country. It is a very "hungry" country. And there was no intent—apologies, perhaps there was intent but no actual procedure—of paying you back that USD 16 (they did pay it back years later).

At the same time, the 2008 global recession, combined with competition growth, brought markets to a situation where the average margin on each flower stem dropped from USD 0.06 (in my case, not including the spray roses under contract) to USD 0.03 (three US cents per stem). This made the additional VAT cost very heavy. Lucky enough, I had the growing contracts, partner farms, and a 30% saving on logistics. At some point, Girish told me that the amount of VAT the government was withholding made the company not very attractive.

I knew there was a way out, I just didn't know what it was, and I needed more time. Time to create something new, or time to come up with a solution, perhaps even both. The VAT application wasn't sudden; we knew it was coming at least a few months in advance, and I had already started research and brainstorming.

This new law primarily affected companies like MAO Flowers because we were not growers/producers but rather middlemen. Growers who produced flowers and exported them directly had no VAT because they were not selling to a local Kenyan company but straight to a client abroad— passing customs. I know what you might be thinking: making MAO Flowers a grower. But that was not easy and financially, not interesting.

At the same time, I was checking the possibility of moving MAO Flowers to another country; this also presented more problems than advantages. Finally, after consulting with accountants, Kenya Revenue Authority

(KRA) people, and Kenya Plant Health Inspectorate Service (KEPHIS), I came up with a solution.

## Exploring the EPZ: A Grand Vision and Practical Hurdles

Just before that, there was one more option on the table: the EPZ (Export Processing Zone). It's a special zone designated and confirmed by the government that attracts foreign businesses and investments on one side and promotes the export of local production on the other. Usually, it refers to raw material that should be processed and then exported to the open world market as a final product.

This zone could physically be at any government-confirmed location, not necessarily at the airport, and it would have its own customs office and officers. After the processing was completed, that officer would come, check the shipment (products) and documents, and then stamp that the product had passed customs. This was true even if the physical location was even 100 miles from the airport. Then, in designated trucks with specific customs seals, the shipment would go straight to the airport terminals' cold rooms, bypassing the customs line, ready to be shipped.

Sounds interesting? Indeed. I loved that idea simply because I love new projects, challenges, and creating solutions for them. But in that case, it was too complicated, and here's why.

First, it would be very costly to set up something like that and get all necessary government approvals. Also, the land where such a complex would be located would need to be designated and converted for that purpose. Establishing such a project would mean creating something like the Amsterdam Flower Auction – Aalsmeer, with a huge facility. That center would process absolutely all, or the majority of, flowers exported from Kenya. Only in that case would it be financially interesting.

This grandiose idea of mine—more than that, MAO Flowers was already doing something similar but in very small volumes for such a project—made me very excited, and I brought it to Girish and more growers' meetings. I was ready and knowledgeable to build and run such an operation, where all flowers from Kenya, and perhaps even Tanzania (with all its problems), would come to this facility, be repacked, quality-controlled, labeled, and exported according to my standards and cost savings. Everybody would win from that, and it was clear to all and not only to me.

Unfortunately, only a few growers agreed to cooperate, and I didn't know where to get investors. To be honest enough, in all my entrepreneurship and business, bringing in capital or the right people was always an issue for me. As my wife, who is an expert in that field, says, "I *was raised by repatriates and was not socializing with the right people."*

She was right.

At the same time, there were a few EPZ zones operating in Kenya. Two caught my attention. One, if I'm not wrong, was in Athi River, and I was told that the PJ Dave Farm, located in Athi-River, past the JKIA airport, wanted to have one as well.

In 2013, the group of farms were operated by the kids and even grandkids of the original owner whom I had a chance to meet in person when I was founding my project in 2006, the old man, PJ Dave. It was a very short meeting on his farm, but I was very impressed by this person, how smart and passionate he was. But the geography of that location was not attractive enough to even start a conversation with them.

The other option was the EPZ zone on Mombasa Road, on its way to the airport, maybe eight miles before JKIA. There were several companies operating from there; one of them was somehow connected to Total Touch Cargo BV Holland (TTC). TTC was working in partnership with Air France and Martin Air. I didn't mention this earlier, but this was the first company I was working with to export our flowers from Kenya back in 2006 and later in 2013. I was told that that TTC had a sub company that had financial struggles and would most likely go bankrupt. So, it was a few years later when I was an advisor at Flowers Business Support Holland (FBS) took over that facility in 2015.

The other consideration of why not, and why I didn't use it later with FBS, was the location. From the first perspective, it seemed like the best place. Mombasa Road in Nairobi is the main road connecting not only Nairobi but also all the farms and all areas from the North East. Sounds great.

In 2016, advising a group of investors, I suggested they not have offices in the same place. It took me time convincing them why not. Kenya, almost like India, is known for its biggest traffic and lack of a traffic light system, together with lax traffic laws in general. When traffic was very bad, many trucks coming from northern farms (70% of the flower farms) would use a very tiny back road to get to the airport. Using that road, located maybe 5-6 miles away from the EPZ, would cause business operation disruptions, flight delays, missing boxes, and the list went on and on. Those trucks would go first to JKIA, offloading other flowers, and only after that, on their way back to farms, would they drop flowers off to us.

I would suggest you remember the rule of a "vehicle garage" that can cost your business success or failure.

*Learned Lesson: Creative Problem-Solving in Complex Tax Environments*

*Navigating challenging tax landscapes requires deep research, consultations with local experts, and a willingness to explore creative structural solutions beyond conventional approaches. While grand visions like consolidated export hubs can offer significant advantages, practical considerations like location, infrastructure, and gaining stakeholder buy-in are paramount. Always consider the hidden operational costs and potential disruption (e.g., traffic, alternative routes) when evaluating seemingly ideal locations, as these can be crucial determinants of success or failure.*

**Reflection and Wrap-up:**

**The bigger your dream, the more rooted in reality your execution must be. Sometimes, the smartest move is not just innovation, but restraint. The tax challenge wasn't just a financial puzzle—it tested vision, ethics, and grit.**

**When systems change, don't resist—rethink. Bureaucracies won't bend to you, but you can outthink them. Sometimes, the best way through is not around, but a step back followed by a smarter leap forward.**

**Your next move:** What regulatory or market obstacle could become a launchpad if you approached it more creatively?

# Chapter 55:

# The Rule of the 'Vehicle Garage' – Micro-Logistics, Macro Impact

## Understanding the "Rule of a 'Vehicle Garage'"

In 2008, I was already familiar with the biggest and most prominent flower companies in Moscow and across Eastern Europe, stretching into Asia. I knew their owners, managers, and physical locations intimately. To truly understand what I call the *"Rule of a 'Vehicle Garage',"* I will provide a few illustrative examples.

After 1992, when the USSR broke apart, the privatization process began. Before that, most or all properties—real estate, farms (known as Kolhoz in Russian)—belonged to the government. This is why, when my parents moved to Israel, we left everything behind and were only allowed to bring USD 130 per person with us.

But with privatization, smart and entrepreneurial young people realized they could make a fortune. This was also the time of "Criminal Russia." They were buying apartments, shops, and factories almost for free, rebuilding them, and renting them out. In 1992, you could buy an apartment near the Kremlin in Moscow for USD 1,000 or a factory for USD 10,000; later, they would cost millions.

Those who were smart, bought or physically acquired these places and land, and some established flower businesses, and we already know why. Others were renting. In the late 2000s, criminal activity was not as open as before but still existed. Good location was in high demand. Some of my flower clients had to re-rent their places and move; some were "asked" to relocate.

I remember a client, a medium-sized business, who relocated his fancy flower shop just three buildings away from its previous location. He used all possible means of advertising and informing his clients about the relocation, but in the first quarter, he lost about 60% of his clients, eventually closing his business by the end of the same year. This happened by moving just three buildings, not even blocks away.

The major reason was the bus station near a subway station. Before, if you were getting out of the subway, just as you hit the last stair, you could see his flower shop. The bus station was also 20 feet away. Even if you weren't planning to buy flowers, while waiting for your bus, or if you lived within walking distance from that subway station, while coming up from the underground, you would remember all the "bad things" you did or said in the morning to your partner/wife/girlfriend, and you would definitely want to fix that gap by buying flowers.

Moving that shop three buildings away created two problems that cost him 60% of his clients almost immediately:

1.  The Factor of Cardinal Directions: While coming up from the subway train, and feeling all the guilt and possible mistakes you made in the morning, you would still consider one last critical mistake. If you weren't going straight home from that station and getting there late, you'd probably be judged and accused of having an affair. The point is that by coming up, if your home direction was west, east, or north from the new location of the flower shop, you would no longer go there. You would prefer to get flowers at your starting point subway station.

2.  The Bus Station Factor: By walking a few more buildings to get the flowers, you would miss and not see an incoming bus, in case you used it to get home from the subway.

This was an example involving a medium-sized flower shop client. The other example is of a major client of mine who relocated to a bigger facility as part of an expansion strategy. His miscalculation was simple—a private vehicle garage near the entrance to the new place.

Imagine a highway taking you up or down the country. You have a flower business—a network of shops. A few times per week, you're sending your trucks to a main city, let's say Philadelphia. You would choose your flower supplier not only based on prices, trust, or sympathy for the owner or manager, but also based on accessibility. How easy and how long will it take your truck driver to get from the highway up to that flower location?

If, for example, after getting off the highway, your driver gets stuck in traffic, or encounters too many traffic lights, or a well-known police station with a "business approach," you might recalculate, and the seemingly lower prices would actually cost you more. Also, remember that your truck would go to different locations to collect flowers and other garden accessories that your shops might sell.

Now, let's go back to my client, the one who expanded. His business was doing well, and he needed a bigger space. Before, after getting off the highway, if your HQ was located north of Philadelphia, it took seven minutes to get there. But after relocation, your driver would have to drive two miles extra, make a U-turn, and go an extra three blocks with three traffic lights because there was a private vehicle garage on a tiny street that did not allow your truck to make the safe turn.

## External Factors That Can Make or Break Your Business

Here is a short list of external factors that might affect your business that I believe you should know. If you're already a pro, remember this: A student saying to a master, *"I already know it and am implementing it."* A Master would say, *"Thank you for reminding me."*

- Road condition and accessibility: Is the path to your location smooth, or does it involve potholes, narrow turns, or other hindrances?

- Type and number of stairs or lack thereof: Is it friendly for four seasons? This includes local government policies on accessibility.

- Distance from and list of nearby competitors: How does your location position you against rivals?

- Type of windows: Do they offer good visibility and natural light?

- Quality of light and adjustments that could be made: Can your space be optimally lit for your product or service?

- Natural environment (trees, bushes): In security, we call it Crime Prevention Through Environmental Design (CPTED), but it's equally well-applied in business strategy for visibility and flow.

- Public transportation: How close are bus stops, subway stations, or tram lines?

- Parking: Is there ample, convenient parking for customers and deliveries?

- Restaurants: Are there amenities nearby that might draw traffic or serve your employees?

- Direction of residence, sunset, and sunrise: How does the sun affect your signage or customer experience at different times of day?

If you still haven't noticed, most of this book is based on risk assessments, risk mitigations, and business strategies sourced from security, all coming together to form one simple method that I call, **"Look. Listen. Respond."**

Finally, the last option or potential opportunity was with Air Connection, where I had Ultra Flo offices before. From conversations we had, when the threat of VAT became real, Air Connection was considering creating such a zone at their facility, and even the land sounded like it could be approved. But after long conversations without a clear direction, the idea was dropped as well.

### Learned Lesson: The "Vehicle Garage" Rule and Micro-Logistics

*The "Rule of the 'Vehicle Garage'" emphasizes that seemingly minor, external logistical or environmental factors can have a disproportionately large impact on business success. Accessibility, visibility, traffic flow, and even pedestrian behavior patterns around your physical location are critical strategic considerations, not mere inconveniences. Businesses must "Look, Listen, and Respond" to these micro-level details to mitigate risks and capitalize on opportunities, understanding that location advantages are dynamic and influenced by a myriad of often-overlooked variables.*

**Reflection and Wrap-up:**

**Big business strategy often lives in the small details. Before you blame your product, team, or market, zoom in on the overlooked: the routes, lights, stairs, turns, signs, and schedules.**

**Micro-logistics shape macro results. Don't just think big— think close. Zoom in on your surroundings. Your success might depend less on what you do, and more on what you didn't notice.**

**Your next move:** What "garage-sized" obstacle might be quietly undermining your business? Look again.

# Chapter 56:
# AI 2025 – The CoTech Era and A New "I"

## From Past Solutions to Future Realities: The Rise of AI

Before giving you the solution for the VAT I came up with, I want us to transfer to the future from there. The future that today is our reality. It is the year 2025, and AI is growing very fast. My, **Look. Listen. Respond** method has advanced since then, and I am teaching and speaking for corporations and running seminars. I also came up with two new terms that I continue to develop with my wife, Patricia: the #CoTech Era and the #ANI.

### The CoTech Pandemic

CoTech describes the dual impact of COVID-19, snowballed together with the effects of evolving and further integrated technology into our day-to-day lives. Together, they've shifted the web of communication, mental health, and societal behavior—our cultural DNA. It has also blurred the line between facts, humanity, machines, and trusted sources.

Today, children as young as seven are now required to have smartphones in schools in high-income countries like Israel. In the US, kids typically receive their first smartphone between 10 and 11 years old, with this age dropping. Forty-two percent of children 8 or younger in the U.S. have their own tablet devices, according to Common Sense Media. While this ensures connectivity, it also creates dependency, disrupted focus, eroding critical thinking that requires sustained attention, and lesser human interaction. This report focuses on a need to refocus on a human-centered approach to combat key emergent business challenges.

## ANI: A New "I" in the Age of AI

ANI isn't just a concept—it's a call to realign on humanity and its healthy interaction with technological advancements. As AI evolves, ANI emphasizes evolving or re-instated empathy, communication, and connection, offering a chance to address the imbalances amplified by the CoTech pandemic—impacts that we've only begun to see as younger generations merge with tech, deeply integrated into their lives.

For leaders, ANI drives corporate resilience. A 2022 Gartner HR survey of 230+ HR leaders found a 37% increase in employee engagement under "human leaders," with engaged teams performing 27% better. Human leaders are defined as Authentic (purpose-driven, fostering self-expression), Empathetic (genuine care for well-being), and

Adaptive (flexible, meeting unique team needs). *Yet, only 29% of 3,400 surveyed employees felt their leader embodied these traits.*

You can find our full report by visiting my website or LinkedIn profile. But I can make it simple. As mentioned, CoTech is a combination of the post-COVID-19 era with technology advances. ANI stands for A New I. Together, it leads to a very simple, yet difficult-to-answer question hidden in the message: *Who is A New I,* or *who am I in this post-COVID, technology-driven world?*

Is our society ready for such a fast change? How will the new generation of leaders—those graduating now or even our kids, who will graduate in 10 years from now—think?

I was born in 1978, "an old generation" that had the chance and the opportunity for critical thinking, real-life experience, and values passed to me by generations of my grandparents. That makes us more resilient and better able to analyze things, thoughts, situations, and life.

Will our kids, who are spending 80% of their time locked into their smart devices, asking for answers from not-yet-fully-developed machines that lack emotions, empathy, sympathy, or feelings to give correct answers? What will the decisions made by those kids look like in the future?

AI is a very helpful tool, but along with that tool, or even more importantly, other perceptions and methods—real-life tools—should be developed and taught to our kids.

Reflecting on this book and the lessons I am passing on based on my experience, it's easy to see that in many cases, actions and decisions involved humanity, critical thinking, "smelling the environment," and feeling the pain of people, customers, something that machines at least for now, cannot provide.

Why am I telling you all this? Simply because changes happen so fast, technology is adopting and growing at the level of self-learning, and threat systems will replace people. Yet, I believe that such ideas and solutions could not be made by AI. The system perhaps could or will be able to provide advice based on uploaded data, analyzing it very fast, but it is your call, your creativity and experience, your ability to read the room that will make  change.

### Learned Lesson: Human-Centered Leadership in the CoTech Era

*The accelerating integration of technology (CoTech) necessitates a renewed focus on human-centric leadership (ANI – A New I). While AI provides powerful analytical tools, truly impactful solutions, resilience, and effective leadership continue to stem from critical thinking, empathy, and the ability to "read the room"— qualities currently beyond the scope of artificial intelligence.*

*Future success will depend on cultivating these human attributes alongside technological proficiency.*

**Reflection and Wrap-up:**

The more sophisticated our tools become, the more vital it is to return to the basics—our senses, instincts, and humanity. Machines may predict trends, but they cannot feel the pulse of a room, or the silence after a bad decision. We must redefine intelligence not just as data mastery, but as human wisdom.

We're no longer just building businesses—we're shaping how future generations interact with life, tech, and each other. The CoTech era isn't something to fear, but to navigate consciously. Reclaim your "I" in this age of AI. Don't let your leadership be outsourced to code.

**Your next move:** Ask yourself—not your phone—who do you want to become in this new era?

# Chapter 57:
# Creative Tax Avoidance and Geopolitical Storms

## Avoiding VAT Legally with Creativity: A New Business Model

I called this chapter "creativity" because I truly believe that in many cases, solutions are born not just from compliance or regulation, but from creative adaptation. That was true when I founded a legal MLM structure in Israel at 22, again in my food business years later, and especially during a turning point in Kenya.

*Quick recap: The Kenyan government imposed a 16% VAT on horticulture and perishable exports, previously tax-exempt. That meant farms added 16% to the price of goods, while export companies like MAO Flowers, which bought and sold locally before exporting, became subject to VAT without timely reimbursement.*

After ruling out the Export Processing Zone (EPZ) model and other large infrastructure solutions, I did something simple but profound: I stopped exporting. Sounds dumb? Maybe. But it worked.

Instead of owning and exporting the flowers, MAO Flowers transitioned into a service provider. We helped foreign clients—many of whom didn't speak fluent English or understand the local landscape—by acting as facilitators, not exporters. We:

- Allocated their orders with farms

- Performed quality control at the airport

- Repacked as needed

- Arranged export documents

- Handled logistics end-to-end

By shifting the ownership of goods and reframing our business model, we legally avoided the VAT. We never owned a single stem, and therefore never sold anything locally. That model, based on trust, documentation, and sharp logistical design, is still in use today in my advisory roles.

## Maidan Square: Bullet Holes in a Wall

While adapting to taxation policy changes, another storm hit: geopolitical instability in Ukraine.

In early 2014, I had just returned from Kiev and Dnepropetrovsk, meeting major clients like UkraFlora and Victoria Flowers. Around that time, I began noticing delays and confusion regarding their Women's Day orders—something highly unusual.

What unfolded next became known as the Maidan Uprising. From February 18–20, violent clashes erupted in Independence Square (Maidan), killing over 100 protesters and several police. The president fled, and civil order dissolved. Russia soon annexed Crimea.

The implications for business were immediate:

- Supply chains were paralyzed. Borders closed, trucks stopped, risk soared.

- Markets froze. Consumers weren't buying flowers amid chaos.

- Political players disappeared. Contacts vital to operations vanished overnight.

I still flew to Kiev a week later to meet remaining clients. My hotel was farther from Maidan than usual, and when people asked what I saw, my answer was simple:

*"Bullet holes in the walls. Barricades in the streets. Unmarked soldiers. Tourists taking pictures. A beautiful, terrifying mess."*

I made sure I had backup plans for evacuation and knew how to contact the embassy. For the first time, I didn't even shop for local goods to bring back—I just wanted to get out safely.

*Learned Lesson: Adaptability, Legal Creativity, and Geopolitical Risk Management*

*Facing major regulatory changes, like unexpected VAT impositions, demands creative and legal restructuring. At the same time, you must remain alert to external risks that can cripple operations, such as political unrest or war. Success lies in your ability to Look. Listen. Respond. in real-time—and to shift your model before the market, or the system, collapses.*

## Reflection and Wrap-up:

**True leadership often emerges in the quiet between crises—where one decision can make or break your future. What looks like surrender (e.g., no longer exporting) can actually be strategic retreat for long-term sustainability. Creativity isn't just a gift; it's a necessity when the rules of the game suddenly change. In business, as in warzones, survival depends on your ability to sense what's coming before others do and reshape your strategy with speed and integrity. Don't wait for perfect conditions—build with what you have, where you are, and rethink what you thought was non-negotiable. That's where resilience lives.**

# Chapter 58:
# Garlic vs. Airport Customs – The Scent of Observation

## Childhood Memories and the Quest for Comfort Food

Each of us has a childhood memory. That includes food. You know, the French toast that Mom was doing, the scrambled eggs by Auntie, a pancake by Grandma's recipe, or cottage cheese the old-fashioned way. I also had many of those. In Israel, with almost a 10% Russian-speaking population, we had most of the food I used to eat and grow up with as a child. Here are just a few favorites that were very much missing in Kenya back then and even in 2022:

- Homemade cottage cheese: Not the one you can get in a supermarket, but the one made by a grandparent, from fresh milk, boiled and drained, hanging in the kitchen in a cheesecloth.

- Russian dumplings: My wife says there's nothing in common with an Asian one, but I think they're close. Russian dumplings have different fillings: beef, cottage cheese, Siberian style with a mix of beef, pork, and lamb, mashed potatoes, and cherry. Yum!

- Russian sour cream: Like my son usually says, "Oh Man!" When I met my wife, she didn't like any of those, but today she secretly admits that Russian sour cream (from a Russian grocery store in NJ, USA) is much better than the local one.

Anyway, back to me, to Kenya, and business.

There was a lack of food diversity until, I would say, 2018 or 2019. Few supermarkets existed; the biggest was Nakumatt. If you ever traveled to Kenya before 2020, you could see a big supermarket with elephant statues at its entrance. Although there was a lack of food that I liked, I learned how to make all those myself. First in 2015, for family needs, later as a small production supplying the Russian-speaking population in Nairobi, and later in 2022, I founded the Taste Of Home production and distribution company. There, we received 9 out of 10 scores for our food from major chefs, and the biggest hotels were using our food for international guests and events.

Now you know how serious I am about childhood food. Every single trip I made to any part of the world where I could get good food, I always had an extra luggage bag, and thanks to the Turkish Airlines Miles & Smiles Elite program and my crazy amount of earned miles, I could have had even two more extra luggage bags that would always be full of food on my way back to Kenya.

## The Stinky Strategy: Outsmarting Customs with Garlic

This might actually be a funny story about food customs, body language, and applying **"Look. Listen. Respond."** Almost every tourist who has been to Kenya might say that many government officials, such as police, customs, and city council, are always "hangry" and wouldn't mind an extra "meal," especially if you, as a foreigner, did something "wrong" based on their hunger level.

In my case, it was a bit too much food passing through Kenyan customs. From my observation, I knew how they operate, what they look for in your luggage, and how to work around it. Just to be clear, I did not bring anything wrong or illegal, but getting stuck in customs for eight hours negotiating the level of my innocence and the level of their hunger was not my top priority.

I love garlic pickles. Something from my childhood in Moscow, usually made by a Georgian recipe and sold by grandmas in local markets. I tried to make it in Kenya, but this is one of the only few projects I failed. Later, I was told that the problem was the wrong type of fresh garlic. Anyway, that garlic is amazing in taste and terribly strong in scent—stinky, I would say. No, to be correct, stinky almost like used socks that an athletic runner would wear for a week without changing them. Sorry for the details.

My twin girls got a bit older, and their good taste changed in a good way, meaning they liked similar food as I did. Therefore, their demand and my supply were growing. On one business trip, I bought 2 kg of such garlic. Beforehand, I bought hermetic boxes from the supermarket and a lot of wrapping paper, hoping it wouldn't smell. Keeping it in a hotel room refrigerator was the worst idea. For the last two days, no cleaning services were on the same floor where my room was. I should use this as a security tip: to keep your opponent far from your door, keep Georgian pickled garlic.

It was time to fly back home to Kenya. The 2 kg of the snack was not the only food I got there. My fear? Kenyan customs. I knew that upon arrival, they would ask to open my hand luggage and the middle-sized luggage—exactly the one with food. This is where my long-term observation— what I call **Look**—came in. Every time I was flying back to Kenya, I had more than enough time to observe their activities, behavior, and conversations.

After a 10-day intensive business trip, I did have a few pairs of socks that could be very useful. Packing that garlic in the middle of my luggage, putting a few pairs of unfolded socks and, sorry for the details, clean underwear on top of it, together with a minor hole in the package that was keeping the garlic, did the job. I wish I could have filmed it on my phone!

Try to imagine: You, as a potential "ATM," arrive at JKIA, Nairobi, with three or four pieces of luggage, immediately attracting the attention of decent, "hungry" people who work there. But then, the magic moment.

**Boom!**

No, that is not a security situation or attack. It is a Kenyan airport Customs representative opening your luggage that has been in travel for more than 20 hours in different weather conditions, and on top, that agent sees and smells the garlicky socks and underwear! Trust me, he did not have any desire to lift it and check what was under it or how much different food I had brought from abroad. Most of the agents left and went to their office to have a "tea break." Green light, guys! Almost everyone who was there with me used that green light custom corridor.

Now, back to Ukraine. The story above was not just to explain how important traditions and food are to me, and how bad the situation there was if it caused me to skip that tradition and avoid local food and souvenir markets. But also to show how **Looking**—in this case, at customs activity—can be helpful. Many of us while traveling, wait in airports for security screening, passport control, getting luggage, and then going through customs. If you are a regular traveler, you have more than enough time to observe their activities and draw conclusions. Just to clarify, this is not a call for any criminal or illegal activity; if you act within the law such observation in some countries can save you time and money.

*Learned Lesson: The Power of Observation
and Creative Disruption*

*The anecdote of the garlic pickles at customs vividly illustrates the power of deep observation (Look) and creative, unconventional problem-solving (Respond) in overcoming seemingly intractable logistical or bureaucratic challenges. Understanding human behavior, even subtle cues, can provide significant advantages, proving that not all solutions are complex or financial. Even in seemingly rigid systems, a keen eye and imaginative application of available resources can pave the way for smoother operations.*

**Reflection and Wrap-up:**

**Traditions, food, and culture shape our identities and experiences—especially in unfamiliar environments. Preserving those connections becomes an act of resilience, and creativity turns minor obstacles into opportunities. From garlic pickles to bureaucratic bottlenecks, our tools remain the same: awareness, strategy, and a sense of humor.**

**When you travel or run a business globally, it's not just about rules and logistics—it's about patterns, people, and presence. In customs or in life, if you observe closely enough, solutions often come wrapped in something**

unexpected. Like garlic, sometimes the strongest tool in your kit is also the stinkiest.

**Your next move:** Look around. What *"garlic"* can you strategically deploy to navigate your next challenge?

# Chapter 59:

# The Post-Maidan Direct Shock – Information Over Capital

## Flowers in Crisis: Unpredictable Market Shifts

*Reliable information—delivered quickly and clearly—is more valuable than capital.*

I've mentioned earlier in the book that flowers are a very unique product; people buy them in joy and in sorrow. I've witnessed many times that when a political event, an actor's passing, or a major incident/disaster occurred, people would buy more flowers than usual. As a chain, our clients would order more. Of course, it depends on the occasion. People wouldn't buy roses if there was a major terrorist attack in Europe or Russia; in that case, there would be less demand for celebratory flowers and more for Carnations, Chrysanthemums, or even Gerbera. But, if there were significant local or country-wide achievements, then yes, roses would be more in demand during that short period.

Whatever happened on Maidan in Kyiv, Ukraine, was an extraordinary and unpredictable market change. Despite and unfortunately, many lives being lost, the market responded in a different way. Almost immediately, many clients stopped orders. Not only from us, but from everywhere. I was always in good contact and had respectful relationships with most of our competitors. Often, after international Flower Expos, we used to hang out together, a kind of after-party. I remember talking not only to them but also with airlines, truck companies, and handling agencies—everyone who could be involved in supplying anything to Ukraine.

I learned this the hard way: in high-stakes moments, it's not your pitch deck or fundraising skills that save you—*it's the quality of information you have at your fingertips.* Not the data that trickles in when it's too late, but the kind you can gather fast, from multiple trusted sources, in a way that cuts through noise and doubt. If there's one lesson I want you to walk away with from this chapter, it's this: **Reliable information—delivered quickly and clearly—is more valuable than capital.** In a crisis, capital might buy you time. But good information? **It buys you clarity—and that can change everything.**

This time, I could not rely only on my experience and gut feeling; I needed to dig deeper. I had to consider planted flowers, contracts, shifting markets, prices, ordered capacity on aircraft, airfreight prices, flower prices. In addition to what would be in fashion next due to the circumstances, what my customers would do instead of the flower business, how it would affect the global flower industry, payments, debts, and the impact on the fashion and cosmetic industry, which would indirectly affect horticulture.

Straight away, I lost all my clients from Ukraine. And not just me. At that time, many Kenyan growers were already working with clients directly in parallel, or through other third parties—my competitors. That situation was the same in Ecuador, Colombia, Holland and to some extent, in Israel—the major flower suppliers.

Flower growers suddenly got stuck with massive production of flowers. Flowers that were "pinched" (cultivated to be ready) for Women's Day. Flowers are not soil; you can't just store them and speculate on prices. Flowers keep deteriorating every minute; they need to be watered, treated, harvested, packed, and then...? Growers refused to reduce prices. At the same time, some countries came with a position where demand for reduced prices, or "we cancel orders," was almost a demand rather than a negotiation. I had clients from Romania, Belarus, Kazakhstan, and even a customer in Australia who postponed orders. It was obvious that the Aalsmeer Flower Auction prices should drop significantly, and if not there would be more than enough flowers and suppliers with excess volumes who would satisfy orders at the last moment. For me, it was clear that the direct impact was just the first wave; the next would be indirect, a chain reaction.

## The Post-Maidan Indirect Shock: Economic Restrictions and Collective "Punishment"

Later in 2014, Russia was blamed for whatever happened in Ukraine. Again, I am not going into any political or factual research discussions in this book. The information is based on my business observations, communications with multiple stakeholders in the industry from different countries, and news at the time sourced in three languages: English, Russian, and Hebrew.

A few months after the Maidan events, instability in Ukraine hit its highest level. Usually, during middle and low-level instability, there is no major effect on the fresh-cut flowers industry; sometimes sales even increase. People who are financially stable but feel stressed would usually and historically, in those countries, buy more flowers and food (dining out). As I mentioned before, the Ukrainian market was lost, at least for a year. To be honest, big clients usually bought on credit. One more thing that you should know as a risk: **review and mitigate it.**

By 2014, the credit line to this client market averaged 150 days, and that's if you were lucky. Just for your understanding, if you're just starting your entrepreneurial journey: a client getting an order (goods) from you for, say, USD 50,000, would pay you after 150 days, and I cannot promise it would be fully paid. They might pay only 25-30% of their debt.

That's another story that perhaps needs a separate chapter. There were many tricks, blacklists, and techniques that they—the clients—used, and if you are not prepared and skilled, you might lose a lot, perhaps even everything you have built. Business is not for emotionally weak people.

After the situation in Kyiv, the West and Europe applied economic sanctions on Russia. First, the foreign exchange rate between the local currency, the Ruble and the USD, almost tripled itself in a very short period. Before 2014, 1 USD was about 35-40 Rubles; the Euro was not very far from there. But then, suddenly and very quickly, it went up to 130 in some places. It also became hard to buy foreign currency. Since those countries were importing goods, the purchasing price was mostly in USD or Euro. If a single stem of flower before 2014 was 35 Rubles (USD 1), now it would cost 130 Rubles. Imagine what implications this had not only on the flower industry, but also on entire markets. Everything that was imported, and later , everything that was produced locally had its production cost depend on imported parts, accessories, and so on.

Almost straight after coming back from Kyiv, I was already on my way to Russia, meeting major clients starting from Siberia to Moscow. As before, I would emphasize using my methods of **Look. Listen. Respond.** both in business and in this case, also for personal safety and security. Listen to clients, markets, people on the streets, and buyers in grocery shops. I remember spending a few days just walking around from very fancy supermarkets to local, small ones, mostly for people with low income. Those people like to talk. Talking to you, talking with their friends and family members who went with them for shopping, and definitely talking on the phone, emotionally sharing their feelings and observations.

Some of you who have never seen me in person or my picture (here's your chance, visit my LinkedIn profile: https://www.linkedin.com/in/yuly-grosman/), I do not look like a typical Russian person, neither as an Israeli. People in Russia usually confuse me with a tourist who doesn't know the language. It is actually very helpful in such circumstances where you want to get true information or an honest opinion.

The **Listen** part is very important. It provides you with raw information for your market and business tendencies. Based on that information, you can adjust your Business Continuity Management (BCM), which also involves Risk Assessment and Risk Mitigations. If you are new to this business life, you should understand how critical this is. Even if you are a small or medium business, risk assessment and BCM are critical and form the core of your business and actions.

### Learned Lesson: Information as the Ultimate Currency in Crisis

*In times of crisis, prompt access to high-quality, multi-sourced, and unfiltered information is more valuable than capital. Geopolitical events can trigger immediate market shocks and cascading indirect impacts (e.g., currency devaluation, import cost spikes, credit risk escalation). Effective crisis management and business continuity depend heavily on proactive "Look. Listen. Respond." methods, even if it means gathering insights from unconventional sources like street conversations. Understanding and adapting to such rapid shifts, even in volatile regions, is paramount for survival and for mitigating severe financial risks like extensive credit debts.*

### Reflection and Wrap-up:

Crises don't wait for perfect data. Often, your survival depends on your willingness to observe the details others overlook, ask uncomfortable questions, and act on imperfect—but timely—information. It's not about panic; it's about preparedness. What separates resilient leaders from reactive ones is how quickly and deeply they tune into what the world is really saying.

Markets can collapse overnight. Customer bases can vanish in a single headline. And entire industries can shift without warning. But what remains in your control is how you gather, interpret, and act on information. Don't underestimate the power of listening well and moving fast. When the next shock comes, it won't be capital that saves you—it will be clarity.

**Your next move:** Upgrade your information sources. Develop your own informal intelligence network. In volatile times, it's not just what you know, but how fast and who you hear it from.

# Chapter 60:
# The Art of Perception – Beyond Data Sheets

### Grounding Leadership in Reality: The Customer's Pain Point

I like simplifying things, and I like bringing people, especially at a senior level, to reality. And the reality is this: every morning, no matter what title is written or embroidered on your business card or LinkedIn profile, it does not matter what car you or your spouse are driving, you most likely wake up in your pajamas, or other home/night-time clothes, or without. You go brush your teeth, make coffee, read the newspaper, listen to news, check emails, or make breakfast for your kids. This routine is almost the same for all of us. During that time, you listen to information, see things—but do you really perceive them? Noticing nuances?

*Let's imagine you are a tech startup working on a new type of customer care chatbot. You might have an entire division of advisors, marketing strategists, and researchers collecting data about customer satisfaction. This time, you try to be that customer. Check online about companies who use a ready product—a chatbot. Try to be their client. Create a scenario in your head, but it should be a very realistic one. One that will put you at a certain risk with a pain point—a punishment. For example, and depending on your wealth, you could agree with your child, friend, or neighbor that you are going to call the customer care of your bank, DHL, Amazon, or any other company where you are a client, and pretend that there was an identity theft on your account. Agree that every 10 seconds from the moment you start that game and communicate with customer care, you transfer (lose) an amount of USD to this friend—non-refundable. You can start with USD 50, or USD 1,000, or USD 20,000; again, based on your level of wealth. The point is to create a reality—a stressful situation where a normal person who will benefit from your technical solution will resolve their problem of identity theft fast and easily. And if your system is not fast and friendly enough, that person will lose all their money while waiting for the system to reply. I can guarantee with high certainty that after playing this game for four minutes, losing thousands of dollars, you will start to feel that stress, frustration, and anger that your final potential client will.*

Just recently, I was working on my article *"Hidden AI Risks BCM Leaders Must Prepare for Now"* for **Disaster Recovery Journal** about aggression caused by chatbots. I was reading different research and contacted several researchers who argue that chatbots are actually very helpful, saving time, money, frustration for customers, and increase customer satisfaction. Some even suggested that such systems reduce aggression due to the fact that there is no human interaction and feelings involved. During that conversation, I asked those people to share how those researches were conducted. Almost everyone shared that it was based on polls, questionnaires, and even a few lab tests where people were given questions. Sometimes, those sample groups of people were connected to monitors, and they responded. All of them were in a comfortable zone. None were in real-life scenarios with urgency and risk, perhaps even risk for life or health.

The point of this example and others is that by listening to markets, people, your clients—but listening to what they say and feel in their real lives— will make you grow faster, bigger, and bring real impact to this world.

## The Tactile Experience: Lessons from Food Packaging

Another example comes from my food production business. At the beginning, while I designed the brand and the packaging, my team and I spent almost a week in the field, visiting supermarkets, looking at different packages, brands, and people. *What do they take first from a shelf? How do they hold it? How do they turn it around and read labels? How do they put it in their basket, and what space does it take in a bag, basket, and so on?* Then we talked to some of those people, asking them what they liked and didn't like in that process. It was a **Look** and **Listen** process.

Before the **Respond**, we made some samples. We tried it ourselves—the touch, the sensation, the connection.

Finally, we took it to a market, asking random people to do the same. Based on that data, we responded. We responded with a design, material, and connection almost on a magical level. I remember part of the experience was that we had a rope, a wire, on top of our glass jars. Somehow, it was critical that the rope would go three times around the jar versus twice. It created a better connection with our potential client to the product. Finally, the rope itself—it was critical how our client would like to feel it and hold it in their hand. I remember during the **Look** process, it was noticed that the majority of clients would put the rope back after opening the jar, just before putting it back into a refrigerator. We repeated the **Listen** process, talking to those people.

**Reading the Russian Market: Beyond Sanctions**

Going back to the streets in Russia just after the Maidan. As mentioned earlier, I was meeting clients and walking on streets using the same method that I teach now: **Look. Listen. Respond.** I was listening to people in grocery shops, talking about vacations, prices, politics, friendships, retirement accounts, healthcare systems. Men often talk about their wives, girlfriends, or a combination of both. But this also happens a lot in nightclubs. It was part of my strategy to go to a nightclub, sometimes a fancy one and sometimes a normal one. In both, I found my final (non-direct) clients.

Finally, combining all this heard and viewed information, I came to a conclusion that people would keep buying flowers, but their interest would shift to small-headed ones and fewer flowers in bouquets. It was also noticed, without getting into deep statistics, that the majority of men who had more than one woman at the same time would buy a small and cheap bouquet for their spouses and more expensive flowers for their mistresses.

Another critical piece of information I got from the market was about money transfer capabilities. Despite official reports of blocked transactions and frozen payments due to sanctions, on the street level, alternative routes were thriving. This insight proved vital. One trusted client of mine, Vlad, had a payment of USD 50,000 frozen. But because of our relationship and shared knowledge of workaround systems, he managed to reroute funds and fulfill the transaction—and even later recovered the frozen amount.

The embargo also affected logistics, but not significantly. New ways and roads were found, and flowers always found their way to their markets.

*Learned Lesson: The Primacy of Real-World Observation and Experiential Empathy*

*True market understanding and effective problem-solving stem from direct, immersive observation and experiential empathy, not just theoretical data. Founders and leaders must actively "**Look, Listen**, and **Respond**" to the nuanced, often unspoken, realities of their customers' lives and the broader market environment, even (or especially) in high-stress situations. This hands-on engagement, combined with the ability to discern reliable information from informal channels during geopolitical upheaval, allows for agile adaptation and the identification of subtle shifts in demand, logistical workarounds, and financial flows that are invisible from a distance.*

## Reflection and Wrap-up:

Empathy doesn't come from a spreadsheet. It's earned through exposure. From stress-testing chatbot scenarios to holding a product like your customer would, the path to meaningful innovation lies in perception, not projection. If you want to lead—really lead—you must step into the shoes of those you serve and ground strategy in lived experience.

In this era of data and dashboards, remember that perception—real human perception—is your edge. Whether it's designing packaging or navigating sanctions, nothing replaces the clarity that comes from being close to the ground. Want to move the market? Start by observing it. Then respond—not just with logic, but with lived insight.

# Chapter 61:
# Kenya 2014 and Forward – Adapting to New Realities

## The Shrinking Margins and Shifting Market Demands

For a long time, and I mentioned this earlier, profit and commission went down significantly. By 2014, in the best-case scenario, companies could only expect a USD 0.03 margin per stem. For smaller roses, it dropped even further to USD 0.01 per stem. I want to clarify something from the previous chapter about moving back to small roses. When I first came to Kenya and started that project, Kenya was exporting small flowers to Europe. These were mainly 40cm and 50cm roses, cut at stage 1 or 2, with an average head size of 2cm. After 2014, when the Russian market changed, many clients wanted small roses—short, at 35cm and 40cm, but with a big head. These were the same flowers we had planted for Russian markets back in 2007 and onward, premium varieties with big heads but short stems to reduce the price.

I can't say I was lucky; luck had nothing to do with it. I knew the market, and I knew growers, airlines, and freight agencies. I had access to enough volumes of the newly demanded products, and my packing system allowed me to stay on top. While an average farm was packing 600 stems per box, I could do up to 1350 stems of the same roses from the same farm. You can do the calculations. In addition to that, I knew that my biggest clients would struggle more than the medium and small ones. The large clients had contracts with major supermarkets and hotels, and with the Ruble crash, they lost millions. Imagine you supply for example, Target flowers. Target pays you every 180 days. The price is agreed upon in local currency, not USD or Euro. Suddenly, in a week or two, the debt of USD 600,000 (18 million Rubles) they owe you, becomes USD 150,000 with the new exchange rate.

You might ask about an agreement? Not there, not back then. I remember sitting at my client's office in Moscow over coffee. It was a big flower wholesale company, one of the main ones operating across entire Russia. I asked him, *"S., we had an agreement, we've known each other for years, and trust was the motive for our partnership."* S. gave me the best lesson in my business life. He said, *"Yuly, this is life."* Finishing the coffee with me, we stepped out of his building when a valet parking guy brought him his fancy sports car, and S. went for a private boat trip on the Moscow River with his lover.

It was not the first time a client didn't pay, but it was the first time that such a customer as S. did not pay. **Look** and **Listen** were strongly advocating to change my positions in markets and adjust business strategies.

It was also the beginning of me moving back into security and close contact combat, with my initial experience in the security, training and risk assessments industry

Reading this book, you might have noticed a pattern of always moving forward, adjusting to situations, and calculating risks. Coming back from the last trip, the focus was on tightening up connections with growers since it was clear there would soon be a demand for 35cm-40cm roses. At the same time, I still needed good quality and the best presentation. I also knew that Girish might soon suggest or show a lack of interest. As I already mentioned, he is one of the best agronomists, and flowers from his farms were getting, on average, the best prices in Aalsmeer. He always targeted mostly Europe, and lately, a bit of the Asian markets.

## Nairobi 2014: Driving, Police, and Human Resources

In 2014, Nairobi was already an amazing investment and expat hub. The city became unrecognizable compared to how I saw it at first, and even in 2012. Hotels, restaurants, banks, entertainment, and many others flourished. There was also a significant change in security and crime levels.

Interestingly enough, just yesterday, the day before I am writing this chapter, William, who used to be my driver early on, contacted me by WhatsApp. It's not uncommon. Workers who used to work for you as an expat will, once in a while, contact you—unfortunately, not to ask how you're doing, but with very creative stories, usually ending with *"Please help with money, otherwise someone in the family will die."* Don't get me wrong, it's not that I'm a bad person, and I used to help a lot in many different ways. At the same time, during all these years, I learned to recognize when that help is truly needed and when it's mostly for alcohol, local gambling, and so on. Since I mentioned William, I would like to share a quick story on how I started driving in Kenya by myself without a driver. That was a game-changer where more expats started driving without personal drivers. At the first pages of this book, I mentioned that the book, beyond business lessons, is also for curious people who want to know about the fresh-cut flower industry and a bit about Kenya.

I would divide the driving problems in Kenya into two. The first is crazy drivers, with almost no rules, particularly the matatu and local buses. Matatus are the small taxi vans for 10 to 15 passengers—not sure how many actually fit inside. And the buses are the ones that go far upcountry, both within Nairobi and to Tanzania, and the Kenyan coast. Usually, you see them in movies with luggage on top of the roof, and the Nairobi ones, those creatively and massively designed are much better than any costume for Halloween you can imagine, they have very loud music systems and conductors who are usually flying with half their body outside of the bus. The visual is of a bus with open doors and a person holding the door with one or two hands, hanging in the air while that bus is driving. Those are the craziest ones. They go off-road, under roads, with and against traffic. I always used to say that if you can drive in Kenya, you can drive anywhere. All that in addition to a minor problem: in Kenya, as in the UK, traffic drives on the "wrong" side, at least for me.

The second issue was the traffic police. When they get hungry, usually late morning and around lunch, they would target expat drivers hoping to get more. Having a local driver was very helpful. If the police stopped you, the drivers knew how to negotiate the rate, and also, in many cases, you wouldn't pay anything since you could say, *"This is not my driver, I am not paying for him."*

Once, my driver was arrested. It was a tiring experience, mostly because I refused to pay a bribe. We were driving early morning from Nairobi toward Lake Naivasha, an amazing place if you are a tourist. But my trip was purely business. I was visiting some farms. Actually, "the" farm. It was the Veg Pro Group, a well-known grower with many farms. They grow berries, vegetables, and roses. It might be another interesting business story for another time, but once I brought them a new type of berry from abroad with an idea to grow it commercially in Kenya. Later, our friendship with the berries department manager became so strong that I was buying different types of berries from them, such as strawberries, blueberries, and raspberries, for making wine and jams. Also, mostly for self-consumption until 2022, when I opened a food production company.

Oh! Back to the driver and the police. It was early morning, around 06:30 am, when we were driving through the Great Rift Valley, going all the way down toward the lake. I was sending emails; my driver was busy doing his job. I saw that my driver was driving +/- according to the speed limit, which by the way was not indicated anywhere. But let's say I could assume that such road conditions should be around 80km/h.

We had just reached the bottom of the valley, and I noticed many cars stopped at the side of the road. That was an indicator of a police operation. Next, we were stopped. The police came first to my window; I was busy sending emails and just told him a nice "Hi." Then he approached my driver. This time it took a long time, longer than usual. Finally, my driver told me that the police claimed we were driving 150km/h. Just to be clear, back then, police did not use any speed guns. In the best-case scenario, there would be an "undercover police officer" sitting on a side road, maybe

10 km away from the rest. This guy would "manually" in his head calculate how fast your car would pass from point A to point B, and would come up with your speed. That number would be sent by SMS to the police team 10km forward, together with your plate number, car make, and color.

The officer offered us the classic "quick fix." Pay KSH 30,000 (about $300) and move on. I refused. I've never paid a bribe, and I wasn't about to start.

Over the next 15 minutes, the price went up to $500, then down to $100, and finally settled at $120 with the officer threatening to arrest *me* instead. That is, until they saw my "magical blue card." (Let's just say that story stays confidential.)

In the end, William was arrested and taken to Naivasha Police Station, notorious among expats for being the harshest in the country. Fortunately, I had something few others did — a dashboard camera from one of my other business ventures, recording GPS data and speed.

Even with the proof, I had to pay a court bond of $200 to release William. Months later, he went to court, presented the GPS evidence, and won the case. Six months after that, I got my $200 back.

Back to William. I was avoiding driving by myself mostly because of the police, crazy drivers, and the comfort where I could work in the back seat while someone was driving me. But one day, at around 02:30 am when I was supposed to be on my way to JKIA airport to catch my Turkish Airlines flight to Istanbul, my driver did not come. He also did not pick up his phone. I was waiting up to the last minute, called all of the taxi drivers I knew (Uber started operating much later), but no one was available. I could not ask my ex-wife (wife at that time) to drive me, since our kids could not be alone at home at night. Not in Nairobi!

So, I took the key of my car and drove to the airport. I left my car at my office in the airport, and the keys with security, hoping that my driver was still alive and would pick up the car early in the morning. Some people say I am very tough in business and managing, but I have a very simple belief and rule: People make mistakes, all of us. I also do. But I believe that people should learn from those mistakes, and I give them usually three chances. Someone asked me, *"Yuly, why three? Not five? Not one?"*

To be very honest and clear, and since we already established my belief that everyone makes mistakes, including me, therefore one chance is not enough for a person to realize he did something wrong. After that realization and acknowledgment, one usually can start the process of improvement that might also involve some mistakes on that journey. This process cannot happen if you, as a leader, an executive, do not help. It is our responsibility as executives to highlight the mistake, understand why that person did what he did, then together develop and provide him tools and perhaps extra information that you can call a Special Operation Procedure (SOP).

A year later, I was consulting Wells Fargo Kenya, and that method was very helpful despite HR struggles—not as a department, but mostly because of regulations and strong union presence. Fortunately, my driver was not part of any union, and I was a direct decision-maker. The very next day I came back to Kenya, he reported to the officeand gave back the car keys and I sent him to HR for clearance.

### Learned Lesson: Navigating Volatility with Adaptability and Principled Leadership

*In highly volatile markets with shrinking margins, survival demands extreme adaptability, a deep understanding of local logistics, and creative solutions to unforeseen challenges. The "This is life" lesson from your client S. underscores that while agreements are important, market realities and self-interest can override them, necessitating constant vigilance and a readiness to pivot. Furthermore, navigating complex operationl environments in foreign countries requires understanding cultural nuances, local authorities, and, crucially, a principled approach to managing personnel. Providing employees with multiple chances and the necessary tools (SOPs) for growth, while maintaining clear boundaries, builds a more resilient and effective team.*

Reflection and Wrap-up:

Flexibility is not a luxury in unpredictable markets—it's a survival skill. The experience with S., the Russian client, and with local police in Kenya both reflect how unpredictable systems require not just readiness but responsiveness rooted in values. Adapting doesn't mean compromising integrity.

Business success in volatile environments isn't about luck—it's about deep listening, agile pivots, and ethical leadership. When the environment shifts beneath your feet, the best investment is your capacity to adapt with clarity, courage, and conviction.

# Chapter 62: Splitting Flowers and Expanding Horizons

## Adapting to a New Flower Market: The "Supermarket" Approach

Before I allow myself to step aside from the main book toward Nairobi and its culture, it's time to move back. The 2014 market changes made me prepare several strategies to secure our position. Moving back to the short flowers yet with big heads was one strategy; advancing even more packaging and restructuring the business toward medium and small clients who could pay in advance and were slightly more flexible with prices was another project that needed new strategies.

Even after so many years, since I started the Kenya project and implemented so many changes, most farms and exporters were still selling only full boxes, sometimes even mixing varieties. As a client, you were supposed to order a full box, let's say, of *'Sweetness Rose'* 60cm (260 stems), a full box of *'Hot Blood'* 70cm, and in addition, farms had minimum orders between 2000 stems and 5000 stems per order.

That kept away small clients who could pay cash upfront and collectively order more than a few big clients who also had a greater risk of paying you.

Back then, I was not familiar with Amazon's structure, but the concept of making small client's life and orders easy was close to my next business strategy. Rebuilding and restructuring MAO's order strategy was not hard, finally coming up with a solution where a client could combine their order with a minimum of 100 stems per variety. Almost like a supermarket, where you walk with a shopping trolley and put items inside, making sure the trolley is full. That approach created a chain reaction in the markets. Small clients who didn't want, for example, 100 'Akito' (white rose) found competitors in their markets who would take some with them. My clients themselves created more clients. Our task was consolidating bigger orders from farms at our facility in the airport (our cold rooms). We were doing the quality control, repacking flowers based on orders, preparing documents, securing space on aircrafts, and further logistics up to the final destination, together with predicting and mitigating risks—and most of it would be paid in advance. Of course, we kept some big clients as well, who kept me awake at night and my stress level high.

By the end of 2014, Girish told me that he preferred to step out and close MAO Flowers Ltd. However, later we managed to keep it operating until later and added more business.

## Culinary Ventures: From Personal Craving to Commercial Enterprise

Meanwhile, the expat community grew very fast, and people wanted food they were used to. The same as I. Once, I came back to Kenya, and I "accidentally," found in my luggage an American Sweet Potato that I bought in Israel during one of my visits. The only sweet potato in Kenya that could be found was a local orange or white color, but far from the familiar taste of the American Sweet Potato. Since Girish was also growing vegetables, I asked him if they could try and grow it. A few years later, almost every grocery shop has American Sweet Potato. To be honest, I do not know if it was "ours," but it tasted familiar.

I cannot directly claim that this was also my project, but the idea was there. Talking about business ideas and innovations, I had a few more. Being born and spending the first 12 years of my life in the USSR, I had the opportunity to love Russian food, part of it was buckwheat Kasha (porridge). We consumed it in large quantities and in different ways, starting for breakfast with milk, as well as a side dish with butter, and so on. Years after moving to Israel, we also had it there. The only place we did not have it was Kenya. As you remember from my earlier sharing, my business trips always involved shopping and coming back home to Kenya well packed with good, hit-home food. Bringing back 3-4 kg of buckwheat that was split between myself and my kids was a must. Sometimes when friends visited us, they also started asking where to get it. Years later, in a "Healthy U" shop in Nairobi, we could find buckwheat with an incredible price of USD 10 for 100 grams versus USD 1 for a kg in Russia or USD 2 for 1 kg in Israel. Running a small bit of research, I found out that the only close place in the growing buckwheat were some attempts in Ethiopia and not very successful. Talking to some world-leading agronomists that I already knew, I was advised that Kenyan soil, especially in the Timau area (near Mount Kenya, where they grow wheat), would be ideal for such a project.

Next step? Girish. What I liked with Girish was that he liked new adventures and was ready to try things. And we tried many; some were successful, some not. Did you ever think of growing a Christmas Tree in Kenya? Well, I did, and we even tried. We planted a trial from a Polish Christmas tree breeder. It did well for more than a year. Unfortunately, it was "destroyed" by a farm gardener who decided it was not a tree but a strange rose bush that should be treated accordingly. Even if that trial did not last long, I still strongly believe that such a business project is interesting for the entire region. It is a long-term investment, but the demand is there.

As mentioned, the expat community had grown, so had their appetite and needs. I love everything dairy, and a lot of it. Still, I believe that back in Russia—USSR—sour cream and homemade cottage cheese were the best, and I did try them in many countries with the option to compare. In Kenya in 2014, there was no sour cream, or cottage cheese. So, I started to study how it could be done at home. At the same time, "Russian and Siberian Dumplings" also sat deep in my head. After several trials, combining methods and recipes, I managed to produce amazing sour cream, and using the fact that Girish was also breeding cows at his farms, I could always have access to great and high-quality milk. First months, I was producing only for self (family) consumption. The sour cream, the homemade cottage cheese (the village style where you prepare raw material, then put it in a cotton cloth hanging on a window, finally getting the clear and delicious product), all types of dumplings, and working closely with Veg Pro Growers, on my way back from farms, as mentioned I was getting berries for homemade jams and later on even wine. The best was Raspberry Wine. Back then, I was very sociable, and friends used to hang out with us. Fast enough, they discovered my cooking talent, and that information spread across Nairobi. When Girish first informed me about the future of MAO Flowers, I was already cooking food and dumplings at nights, during the daytime still managing flowers, and on evenings and weekends was otherwiseoccupied. The entire Russian-speaking community, many working in UN Nairobi, were my clients.

Without getting into the details, MAO FLOWERS' export operation went significantly down, but I was already consulting a Dutch Export company in Kenya who wanted me to expand their activity from Kenya and even connect exports from Israel. In 2006, exporting from Israel, I expanded to Kenya. In 2014, the client wanted to consolidate and expand services for his clients with export from Israel. Life is very interesting and unpredictable. One of the trips to Israel, I found a Dragon Fruit exporter that was a main aspect and priority. But since there were big changes in different markets, I could not rely only on that.

### Learned Lesson: Nimble Adaptation and Niche Market Innovation

*Successful long-term business strategy requires constant re-evaluation and a willingness to pivot, especially in volatile markets. Adapting to shifting client demands (e.g., from large to small flower orders, with flexible bundling) can open up new market segments and mitigate risks associated with large, high-credit-risk clients. Furthermore, identifying and fulfilling niche consumer needs, particularly you are within underserved expatcommunities, can lead to unexpected and highly successful entrepreneurial ventures, even those stemming from personal cravings. The consistent willingness to "Look, Listen, and Respond" to both macro-economic shifts and micro-level consumer desires, coupled with a proactive approach to risk and supply chain management, is key to sustained business growth and innovation.*

Reflection and Wrap-up:

When traditional structures don't serve emerging needs, there's room for something entirely new. What began as my personal cravings for sour cream and buckwheat became seeds for ventures that fed a whole community. Sometimes, reinvention comes not from a pivot away from the old, but by listening to your present needs.

Growth doesn't always follow a straight path. It branches out—from flowers to food, from international exports to small-batch dumplings. What matters is your ability to seize opportunity in uncertainty, to stay curious, and to act when others hesitate. Innovation is often just a craving, followed by action.

# Chapter 63:
# Martial Arts and Back to Security –
# A Journey of Resilience

From Injury to Instructor: The Unpredictable Path of a Ninja

I might have mentioned at the beginning of this book that I started my martial arts training in 1991, all the way to joining the Israel Defense Forces (IDF). By then, I had already earned a brown belt (Kyo 2), just two steps away from black. I was excelling—my Sensei Eli used to say, *"Yuly, you are a great Karateka and have a big future."*

Then life, in its unpredictable way, stepped in.

During my IDF service, I sustained an injury that left me a Disabled Veteran.

While I could no longer spar or train in Martial Arts, I found a dedicated Shotokan Karate instructor in Kenya who respected my limitations. Years later, in 2014, I earned my 1st Dan Black Belt from the Japan Karate Association Kenya.

As I mentioned earlier, the lack of professional martial arts schools created a demand. I used that gap by opening one that reminded me of the Saido Karate I was practicing at when I was young. No talking. No sparring for four years—just fundamentals. Inspired by this, I launched Sacura Martial Arts Academy. It started as a dojo but evolved into a licensed body for global security consulting and tactical training.

Within months, we had seven locations across Nairobi. Besides classes, we sold uniforms, hosted workshops, ran exams—it was a full business. Still, I never connected emotionally with Shotokan. My heart remained with Saido and Kyokushin.

Then students began asking about Krav Maga. One, Sunny, said: *"Sensei, you practiced Krav Maga in Israel. Can you teach us?"* That question changed everything. I dove into global research and reconnected with martial art and security mentors. One was Miki, a "Shin Bet" (Shabak – Security Services) retired and former bodyguard to Israeli prime ministers. Another was Master Haliva, founder of Shadow Krav Maga. When I asked Haliva if he could teach me with my physical limitations, he replied:

*"Do you want a belt, or do you want to survive? Everyone has the right to defend themselves."*

That hit hard.

With their guidance, I became a certified Shadow Krav Maga Instructor, later earning my 1st Dan Black Belt. Our Krav Maga classes soon eclipsed karate. One student, knowing my security background in Israel, asked, *"Can you assess my factory's risks?"* That question brought me back full-circle into the security world.

By 2015, my work spanned flower exports, martial arts schools, food entrepreneurship, and corporate consulting. My food company, launched in 2022, was my last personal venture. Due to health and energy constraints, I eventually reduced many of my operations.

Today, I train police, hospitality teams, healthcare professionals, and universities in topics ranging from business continuity to aggression de-escalation. When I step on stage today for a keynote, it all started here—with injury, recovery, and relentless reinvention.

## The Hidden Battle: Overcoming Pain and Addiction

There's one thing I've kept hidden until now and have mentioned earlier as well, but I think it is important.

Since my IDF injury, I've lived with daily pain. After a second surgery in the 2000s, doctors prescribed Oxycontin and Oxycodone. As a disabled veteran, I received a constant supply. But no one warned me about addiction.

Years later, while living in Kenya, still receiving meds from the IDF, I realized: I was addicted. Worse, the more I took, the more pain I *felt*. A cycle.

No, I wasn't lying in the street. I was functional. I ran businesses, led teams. But my attention span dropped.

Patience became scarce. I made a one-day decision—a bad idea without medical supervision. I flushed the rest of my meds. For two weeks, I shook, acted out, and even forced myself to email the IDF requesting another shipment. But I didn't send it.

Later, I used this experience to help others. I also stopped smoking the same way: cold, decisive.

Here's what I learned: You can't quit for others. You'll always find a reason to relapse. But if *you* decide? You can do it. And if you do, I'm here to help.

*Learned Lesson: Resilience Redefined – From Physical Trauma to Purposeful Action*

*True resilience isn't just about surviving external battles—it's about confronting internal ones. From a disabling injury to founding a global security consultancy, this chapter is proof that limits are often illusions. The quiet battle with addiction reminds us that high performers can still struggle—and that real strength lies in choosing change from within.*

*What if your greatest limitation could become your greatest source of power?*

**Reflection and Wrap-up:**

**The road back to strength is rarely a straight line. I never planned to teach martial arts again, let alone start a security firm. I never imagined I'd fight addiction. But**

pain—physical or emotional—can be the catalyst that pushes us to become more than we imagined.

You don't need to wait for a perfect plan. You need a decision.

This chapter is not about martial arts or security—it's about deciding who you want to be when your old identity no longer serves you. Whether you're facing addiction, injury, or reinvention, your greatest transformation will begin the moment you say: I'm ready to fight—differently.

Let resilience be the lens through which you reimagine every obstacle as an entry point into something greater.

# Chapter 64:
# My USA – The Next Chapter

## Starting Over, Again

In 2023, Patricia and I made the decision to move to the United States. She wanted to be near her dad, and we both wanted our son to enjoy the presence of his favorite grandpa. For me, it felt like starting over—again. When I was 12, we moved to Israel, and I started working almost immediately. At 14, I launched my first business. Over the years, I had built a strong presence in Israel and later expanded into Africa, Europe, and the Middle East. I was known in my circles. Now, in the U.S., I was back to knowing no one.

This new chapter wasn't about proving myself. I've never been one to chase validation. Sometimes, I'm highly social at other times, I prefer to sit quietly, observing. But here in America, I found myself with 35 years of experience, but no established network. It was like holding a powerful engine without fuel.

Yet what I do have is this: a lifetime of stories, lessons, scars, and wins that translate into something real. Whether it was the beauty of the flower industry, the chaos of war zones, or the discipline of martial arts, I know how to *Look. Listen. Respond.*

I used to describe myself as someone who helps executives **Look, Listen,** and **Respond** to change with confidence. But I realized, maybe it's simpler than that. Maybe I help people be more human—by learning to *See* better, **Hear** more, and **Respond** with heart.

## My Core Message: Humanizing Business, One Insight at a Time

My work today draws from the deep well of my lived experience. I don't just teach resilience or leadership or risk. I teach what it means to be a whole person in a fractured world. Whether it's understanding risk in an unstable market or helping a leader reconnect with purpose, the approach is the same: sharpen your perception, stay grounded, act from clarity.

This isn't theory. It's what I've lived—from training youth in Nairobi's toughest slums, to de-escalating security threats in corporate boardrooms, to advising startups during political collapse. The common thread? Humanity.

## Projects I'm Proud Of

- Law Enforcement & Special Forces Training: Helping frontline officers go home safe, and deal with stress and aggression more responsibly.

- Executive Coaching: Supporting high-performers through burnout, career shifts, and personal reinvention—sometimes even as couples.

- University Speaking: Giving undergraduates the real-world, tactical skills to navigate life and work.

- Startup & Risk Advising: Coaching founders to navigate risk, read people, and build for uncertainty.

- Youth Empowerment in Kibera: Teaching survival skills to teens facing daily threats of violence, harassment, and poverty.

**Reflection and Wrap-up:**

You don't need a perfect story to start a new one. Coming to the U.S. is another chapter—one where I bring everything I've learned into a new environment. The context changed. My mission didn't.

If you've made it to this chapter and learned something from my story, I thank you.

If I can support you or someone in your circle, I'd be honored.

Check my website for stories and resources—many free, many from the streets, boardrooms, and battlefields. And if you're curious about what it means to *Look. Listen. Respond.* in your world, let's talk.

This book began as a story about flowers. It became one about resilience, risk, and reinvention. Wherever you are, I hope it sparked something real. The next chapter? It's yours to write.

Keep going. Stay human.

*Yuly Grosman*

A Human being

www.yulygrosman.com

Email: ygros1@gmail.com

To see pictures of the flowers and facilities discussed, please scan this QR Code.

# Author Biography:

Yuly Grosman's rare duality—half a life building successful international businesses, the other half leading in dangerous environments—shapes his approach as a high-impact corporate speaker. He transforms how teams lead, communicate, and operate under pressure.

His philosophy, Look. Listen. Respond., distils decades of experience in international business, special forces, and elite bodyguard instruction into three tactical behaviors. These enable leaders to build trust, respond with clarity, and deliver results when it matters most.

Yuly doesn't just share theory; his immersive, story-driven keynotes are built on real-world consequences. He has trained thousands globally, from first responders and venture-backed startups to C-suite executives, providing hands-on leadership insights.

Yuly is a loving father and husband. For fun, he travels and hikes, reads books, attends plays, and spends time with his family.

To have Yuly speak at your program:
https://www.yulygrosman.com/contact

Still have questions? Book a 15-minute discovery call to see how these programs could benefit you:

https://calendar.app.google/5Nt542Am9kUPcKvcA

BSc Security Risk Management
Certified International Bodyguard Instructor
Certified International Shadow Krav Maga Instructor Black Belt 3rd Dan
Certified Security Operational Planning (Analyses Of The Attacker View)
Shadow Jitsu (Koga Ryu) Black Belt 3rd Dan
Shotokan Karate Black Belt 1st Dan
Certified Purchasing & Logistic Manager (CPLM)

www.ingramcontent.com/pod-product-compliance
Lightning Source LLC
Chambersburg PA
CBHW050502210326
41521CB00011B/2288